SPIRIT
of the
WITCH

About Raven Grimassi

Raven Grimassi is a practicing Witch and the author of several books on Wicca and Witchcraft, including the *Encyclopedia of Wicca and Witchcraft*, which was awarded Best Non-Fiction by the Coalition of Visionary Retailers in 2001, and *Wiccan Mysteries*, which was awarded Book of the Year and Best Spirituality Book in 1998. Trained in both Northern and Southern European Traditions, Raven Grimassi is also an initiate of several Wiccan Traditions, including Britic Wicca, Pictish-Gaelic, and Italian Witchcraft. He is currently the Directing Elder of the Arician Ways, and co-owner of Raven's Loft, an Internet store specializing in Witchcraft items (www.ravensloft.biz). He has been a teacher and practitioner of Wicca and Witchcraft for over thirty years, and his former students include authors Scott Cunningham and Donald Michael Kraig. Raven is also an expert on the topic of Italian Witchcraft and is the leading authority on the works of Charles Godfrey Leland in this field. He has appeared on television and radio, is a popular lecturer at festivals and conventions across the country, and conducts a variety of workshops on magic, ritual, and personal power.

SPIRIT

of the

WITCH

Religion & Spirituality in Contemporary Witchcraft

RAVEN GRIMASSI

2003
Llewellyn Publications
St. Paul, Minnesota, 55164-0383, U.S.A.

FIRST EDITION
First Printing, 2003

Book interior design and editing by Connie Hill
Cover design by Gavin Dayton Duffy
Cover photograph © 2003, PictureQuest
Interior art by Kevin R. Brown

Library of Congress Cataloging-in-Publication Data
Grimassi, Raven.
    Spirit of the witch : religion & spirituality in contemporary witchcraft /
Raven Grimassi. — 1st ed.
        p.   cm.
    Includes bibliographical references and index.
    ISBN 0-7387-0338-9
    1. Witchcraft. 2. Spiritual life. I. Title.
BF1566.G737   2003
133.4'3—dc21   2003058814

Llewellyn Publications
A Division of Llewellyn Worldwide, Ltd.
P.O. Box 64383, Dept. 0-7387-0338-9
St. Paul, MN 55164-0383, U.S.A.
www.llewellyn.com

Printed in the United States of America

Dedication

This book is dedicated in grateful recognition to my readers, old and new, whose faithful support allows me to live my bliss as a writer.

Also by Raven Grimassi

Beltane

Encyclopedia of Wicca & Witchcraft

Hereditary Witchcraft

Italian Witchcraft

Wiccan Magick

The Wiccan Mysteries

The Witches' Craft

The Witch's Familiar

Table of Contents

Introduction ix

Chapter One: The Old Ways 1

Chapter Two: In Search of the Witch 9

Chapter Three: Witchcraft as a Religion 27

Chapter Four: Becoming a Witch 51

Chapter Five: The Witch in Moonlight 75

Chapter Six: The Witch in Daylight 91

Chapter Seven: The Tools of Witchcraft 105

Chapter Eight: The Magical Craft 119

Chapter Nine: The Three Great Mysteries 137

Chapter Ten: Deities and Spirits 153

Chapter Eleven: Rituals 169

Chapter Twelve: Some Parting Words 201

Notes 215
Appendix One: Training Exercises 219
Appendix Two: Witches' Altars 223
Appendix Three: Suggested Course Reading 227
Glossary 231
Bibliography 235
Index 241

Come to the woods,
the spirit's calling you.
Come to the Ways,
that the ancients knew,
preserved for you,
come to the Ways.

Come to the woods,
the spirit's calling you.
Come to the woods,
where the Fay run free,
and Old Ones be,
come to the woods.

Come to the woods,
the spirit's calling you.
Come to the Ways,
and tread moonlight paths
to circles danced,
come to the woods . . .

—Raven Grimassi

Introduction

I wrote this book to convey a sense of what is most noble and beautiful in the spirit of the Witch. In doing so I realized that it is difficult to convey in words what is best embraced by direct experience, for there is no better way to truly learn about someone than to spend some time together.

Several years ago I was a weekend guest at a festival gathering of Witches and other earth religion practitioners. Like most of these gatherings, the event was held in a natural setting of trees and forest meadows, removed from the busy hum and buzz of city life. It was a chance to remember and acknowledge the simple and precious gift of life itself.

One night I was invited to assist with a celebration to take place in a clearing surrounded by trees. The only source of light was the full moon filtered softly through the overhead branches of old oak trees. I stood outside a ritual circle of stones marked out upon the ground, and I waited. Before long, like the approach of a drifting mist, several figures slowly appeared from out of the darkness of night and moved toward me. At first there were just a few figures, and then gradually a procession quietly streamed out into the moonlight. The Witches were coming to venerate the old gods of their ancient ancestors.

During the previous day I had seen many of these people in various campsites. Some were dressed in jeans and T-shirts, others in peasant garb styled like the apparel of the Renaissance era. But here in the night, shrouded in soft velvet and cotton hooded robes and cloaks, each person seemed magically transformed. With their features obscured, and faces mostly unseen, all that remained was the simple feeling each person generated.

During the ritual, each person moved and spoke with a reverence and stateliness that bespoke of the inner spirit of the Witch. These were people from different places, age groups, races, and social/economic backgrounds, all united in the veneration of Nature. Their personal differences gave way to the harmony of the commonality, which united everyone there in that circle beneath the moon.

In the pages of this book I will acquaint you with the spirit of the Witch and introduce you to the things that empower Witches in their daily and spiritual lives. Throughout the chapters of this book, the Witch will be revealed as a citizen living and working like all others, as well as a spiritual being who seeks alignment with the natural world. For the Witch is a seeker of balance, and the Witch crosses at will between the realms of commonplace day and the star-filled night.

It is my hope that in revealing the beauty of the Witches' spirituality, the roots of prejudice, ignorance, and religious intolerance will wither away in the harsh light of truth. Not everyone wants to believe in Witchcraft as a viable and healthy religion. Many people remain bound to the inherited stereotypes that have formed their views and opinions. Several years ago I was part owner of a Witch Shop called Raven's Loft, which was located in Escondido, California. During one Halloween season I happened to be looking out the storefront window one afternoon. I noticed a group of young people painting window scenes for the shops along the avenue. There on several of the windows of my fellow merchants were depictions of old hag Witches with green skin, broken teeth, warts, and long matted hair.

I thought to myself, isn't it odd that here, in the twenty-first century, a society that professes to be opposed to racism, intolerance of alternative lifestyles, and the many faces of prejudice, still finds it acceptable to publicly malign a specific religion or group of people through a display of art.

One of the problems is that many non-Witches are not aware that Witchcraft is a religion and a spiritual path. They have been misled into believing that Witchcraft is all about casting spells for personal gain, and that Witches are in league with what Judeo-Christian theology calls the Devil. For most non-Witches, Witchcraft is something far removed from their lives and their awareness, but what they don't realize is that Witchcraft is one of the fastest growing religions in the world today.

As an author I am often presented with the opportunity to travel for appearances at bookstores, conventions, and festival gatherings. This has placed me directly in the center of large numbers of individuals who define themselves as Witches. What I have discovered is that Witches are pretty much the same wherever I've encountered them, from coast to coast.

I've sat with other Witches around bonfires until late into the evening. I've shared meals with them around a campfire, and have had the honor of standing next to them in the sacred space of our ritual circles where we gather to venerate our deities. What I've found are people of a generous nature—loving, hearty, and open-minded people who are calmly tolerant of the beliefs and lifestyles of other people.

The vast majority of Witches I've met over the years have been well-educated, intelligent, and confident people of good character who also possess a strong will and an independent nature. Witches are people who care about the planet we all live on, and who care about the communities in which they live. I've never met a Witch who did not have both an opinion and a desire to share it.

During my travels as an author, many Witches have remarked to me that there is an overabundance of books on magic, spell casting, and the fundamental practices of Witchcraft. They've often asked why we don't have books written entirely on the topic of spirituality in Witchcraft. While I could think of a few books that did contain a chapter here and there on spirituality in the Craft, I had to concede that I knew of no single volume devoted to the topic.

During a meeting with my publisher I mentioned this, and the reply was "Okay, so write one." Being in many ways a typical Aries, I accepted the challenge without giving the matter sufficient consideration. I later reflected back upon the saying "Ask three witches for their opinion, and you'll get four different views." Therefore, for the purposes of this book, I've tried to stay focused on what I believe are the common elements I've personally noted in the spirituality of Witches.

There are some Witches who will not agree with what I've written in this book, and I would be somewhat disappointed and extremely surprised if they all did agree. Whenever one puts humans into the mix there is going to be politics, and Witches are no exception. Knowing there was no way to not find disfavor with one group or another, I decided to simply bring to bear on this project my thirty years of involvement in the Witchcraft community, and all that I've personally discerned from those years.

It is not my intention to present myself as the primary spokesperson for Witchcraft, because I'm not and no one else is either. I see myself as one of many voices, no greater and no lesser than any other voice. My opinions are, however, informed ones and I simply offer this book as a much-needed work of public education.

This book covers a wide range of topics in an attempt to reveal both the religious elements of Witchcraft and the spiritual viewpoint of its practitioners. To that end I have included material related to the cultural, literary, anthropological, and historical connections. Additionally I have presented material related to the oral traditions of Witches themselves. I feel that in order to understand Witchcraft as a religion and a spiritual path all perspectives are of value.

This book looks at the roots of Witchcraft as revealed in the etymology of the earliest references, as well as in the background elements of the earliest tales written about Witches, beginning as early as 700 B.C.E. Even though many of these tales are fictional, it must be noted that when a writer creates a fiction he or she typically uses facts in the general supporting background structure. For example, a contemporary book about an imaginary being wandering the streets of New York would still employ authentic colloquial elements related to the people, setting, and culture of New York. Therefore, it is not unreasonable to assume that such valid elements exist within the tales of ancient writers on Witchcraft as well.

It appears to be a part of human nature to vilify one's enemies. I know that I grew up in the United States hearing that the Russians were an evil race, and I have no doubt that in Russia at that time, children believed Americans were evil as well. I've met a fair number of Russians as an adult and have yet to find one I would classify as evil, or even as a bad or unkind person. Campaigns of vilification only serve to gain unwitting support from the public for the hidden agendas of those who profit by people believing the propaganda.

In order to mislead people, the creators of deception must make the distorted image of the enemy appear reasonable. To accomplish this, the setting must appear natural, as well as the props, conditions, and so forth. In the case of depicting Witches as evil, the same formula had to apply. Therefore the writer would need to incorporate known and accepted elements about magic, ritual tools, and general folklore/folk magic beliefs. In a setting that is familiar to the people of the time, the writer can then depict the Witch as evil, deranged, perverted, or in any manner that suits the surreptitious agenda of the writer.

Ancient writings about Witches and Witchcraft contain a great deal of background material that reflects ethnographical bits and pieces that can be important in separating pertinent fact from intentional deception. I use this material to gain a clearer image of what the people who lived in such times believed concerning the incidental inclusion of specific common tools, props, clothing, expressions, and so forth.

I have incorporated some historical and ethnographical references related to the tools of Witchcraft throughout this book. My purpose was, in part, to bring to light the importance such elements have held for practitioners over countless centuries. Additionally I wished to demonstrate the antiquity and longevity of many components of Witchcraft that contemporary skeptics claim are nothing more than modern constructions.

This book is designed to provide not only an overview of how Witches view deity, but also to illustrate how the Witches' concept of divinity manifests in the cycles of Nature. To that end the book also includes seasonal rituals. Additionally the reader will find detailed material concerning the relationship between various elements of pre-Christian European religion and modern Witchcraft beliefs, customs, and practices.

ONE

The Old Ways

The following story is fictional, but the truth it conveys is real and viable. Many centuries ago there lived a woman who was a great spiritual teacher. She drew many seekers to the teachings she revealed, and around her formed a group of devoted disciples. After many years of study the disciples left and journeyed to other lands, hoping to spread the teachings they had learned.

The years went by and one day the disciples returned and sought out their old teacher. Once they found her, the disciples posed a question to the master. "We have," their spokesperson remarked, "traveled to many lands, and discovered many different teachings that are unlike the ways you have taught us." The master calmly nodded in acknowledgment, and the disciple continued, "Therefore we are confused, so can you tell us what is the true religion?"

The master looked up with a patient smile and replied, "All of the religions of the world are like individual pearls. Each of them formed around a different grain of sand, in different waters, under different conditions." Then the master looked directly at the spokesperson and spoke softly, saying, "But, if you ask me which is the true pearl, I will tell you that none of them are the one true pearl. Instead, the truth is the thread that runs through, holding them together as a necklace, and that is the one truth you seek."

This story illustrates an important truth. When I first taught Witchcraft as a religion many years ago, I began each series of classes with a teaching that I call "The View of Crystal." I placed a very large, oddly shaped piece of crystal on the floor. Then I had the students sit in a circle around the crystal. Next I asked each student in turn to describe what he or she saw in front of their eyes. Naturally each person described the crystal somewhat differently, because the visual perspective of each individual was different, according to his or her position in relationship to the crystal.

Some people described the crystal as being sharp and jagged. Other individuals described the crystal as smooth and polished, covered with beautiful facets. Still other men and women depicted the crystal differently from even these descriptions. So, who was right and who was wrong? What did the crystal actually look like?

In a short time it became clear to everyone that each person was correct in his or her perception of the crystal, but that each individual's "truth" was only a small part of a much larger whole that existed beyond the single view of any one individual. It was also conceded that the "truth" of one person did not negate the truth of another. Everyone simply had his or her personal view and experience of the crystal. In the end we spoke a great deal about the fact that the only way for us all to know the whole truth about the crystal was for each person to integrate the perspectives shared by all of the others.

We joked around for awhile about how odd it would be if everyone in the room were to argue that their view of the crystal was the only true view. We talked about how angry an individual might get about his or her personal view being dismissed entirely by some or all of the other people. It all seemed so clear and simple in that small room with the crystal centered between us, but sadly we knew that in the real world people have hated and killed each other over their personal view of the crystal for thousands of years, and many still do today.

The story of how, when, and why religion formed in human society is complex and comprised of a great deal of speculation mixed with facts. When we study the mythologies of different regions and the rituals of different cultures, it becomes readily apparent that a commonality of thought and expression exists between them all. This is not surprising because human beings essentially reason and create in human ways.

In the myths and legends of various cultures we find deities and spirits associated with the basic needs and desires that all humans share. There are deities and spirits that wield power over life, death, healing, love, fertility, agriculture, hunting, peace, and war. In the beliefs of all human cultures, we find the existence of offerings, prayers, and sacred places, which again express the commonality of human conceptualization.

The differences we find in the rituals that exist in different cultures lie in the way that things are done, and not in the reason. The beliefs we find differ little as well, bearing different labels and descriptions for essentially the same primary and basic tenets. Despite this, the need seems to exist among humans to not only create different religions but also to create different denominations within a specific religion. As a species we seem to expend a great deal of energy focused on what separates us from one another rather than on what unites us.

In the religion of Witchcraft one can also find different denominations called Traditions. Many of them are constructed around cultural expressions such as Celtic, Germanic, Nordic, Italian, French, Hungarian, Basque, and so forth. Other Traditions draw from various outside sources (some of which have no cultural or historic connection) and are called eclectic systems. Some Witches prefer to remain within the purity of their own Tradition and do not explore the truths residing in other systems (perhaps missing an opportunity to expand and enrich their own current beliefs and practices).

In the chapters ahead we will not explore the differences between Witches and their views, because such things do not really reflect the core spirit of the Witch. Instead we will examine the commonality of those things associated with Witchcraft, which appear in the basic rituals, tenets, and practices of the Craft. To understand the spirit of the Witch, we must look at the ways of Witchcraft, which are ever ancient and ever new.

The Old Ways

According to oral tradition there was once a time when people lived in harmony with Nature, venerated the world in which they lived, and understood their purposeful place in the scheme of things. It was a world in which there was no sense of "wilderness" because there was no civilization for comparison. To our ancient ancestors the forests and the caves were simply home.

Early humans lived in small tribes or family groups. The rules for living together were simple and natural. The survival of the group depended upon working together to obtain food, provide protection, create shelter, and ensure survival. Social rules and taboos evolved over the course of time for a variety of reasons. Certain behaviors were expected, some were tolerated, and others were punished. These were all based upon maintaining peace, safety, and harmony within the group.

Our ancestors were hunter-gatherers, collecting edible plants and their fruits as well as killing animals. Every part of everything hunted or gathered was used whenever it was possible, and nothing was ever wasted. Hunters came to respect the animals they hunted, and a primitive belief arose through which the spirit of the slain animal was honored.

In some cultures, both in Europe and North America, it was a common element of the "rituals of hunting" to eat the warm heart of a slain creature, which in most cases was a deer or some other horned animal. This act was usually performed in a primitive belief that the power and courage of the animal would pass into the hunter. Some modern hunters still perform this act as a rite of passage when killing their first prey.

In Witchcraft this basic magical concept would fall into the category of "contagion magic." It is an old teaching that when any thing comes into contact with another thing, an exchange occurs between the two. A mundane example is putting a sugar cube in a cup of hot tea. The sugar cube then becomes liquid like the tea, and the tea becomes sweet like the sugar cube. They have, in a sense, become like one another.

Living in the heart of Nature allowed people to remain in contact with the vitalizing essence of a natural environment. This vital essence is one of the reasons why modern people feel refreshed from camping in the woods for a few days. Places have an aura or energy field that can cause humans to feel a certain way, which is why we pick a particular spot to camp in, or even a place to sit down on. It simply "feels" right to us at the time. Cities and buildings also have an aura, and make people feel a certain way.

Because buildings are lifeless objects, they absorb energy rather than cleanse and renew it as do trees, meadows, and other natural settings. The artificial places created by humans tend to deplete our energy and are burdensome to our spirits. In a subconscious attempt to offset such influences, people have brought plants and animals indoors, and often surround homes and various buildings with grass and trees. Unfortunately this attempt to pretend that we are still living in the woods is weakened by the asphalt, concrete, metal, and stucco that absorbs and binds natural energy.

For the Witch, maintaining a vital and living connection to the spirits of Nature is of great importance. This is accomplished in several ways. The first step is in establishing a rapport with one's deities as well as the spirits of Nature (however one chooses to define such things). It is an ancient teaching that every natural object contains within it a spark of consciousness from "The Source of All Things." One of the words used for this type of consciousness was the word *numen*.

A numen was believed to be a spirit that inhabited an object or presided over a specific place. As the concept evolved it came to be viewed as a consciousness or spirit within all things, which gave power to the forms in Nature. Eventually the numen concept was transformed into the minor gods and goddesses who were once simply the spirits of woodlands, rivers, streams, and other aspects of Nature.

Rapport with one's deity and the spirits of Nature keeps the Witch within the flow of energy that vitalizes the natural world. By extension the Witch will also develop a rapport with an animal such as a cat, which can serve as his or her familiar. The familiar in animal form is a link to the natural world from which the familiar is less removed than the civilized human. This relationship is also part of the contagion magic principle as earlier defined.

The second step for the Witch is to work with plants. This can be as simple as keeping a few potted plants in one's home, or as elaborate as maintaining a classic outdoors English garden. Growing and caring for plants helps establish and retain a relationship with the spirit of Nature. For the Witch, the world of Nature is divided into realms that are often referred to as the Plant Kingdom, the Animal Kingdom, and the Mineral Kingdom.

The three realms are points of conjunction that help the Witch to maintain his or her connection with the soul of Nature. Traditionally the Witch is united with the Plant Kingdom through herbalism. He or she is united with the Animal Kingdom through the familiar spirit or power-animal, and to the Mineral Kingdom through the use of crystals and stones of all varieties.

The third step for the Witch is the performance of rituals linked to the seasons of Nature, as well as to the phases of the moon. It is an old teaching that "like attracts like" and to be like something is to move closer to being of the same nature as the thing itself. The seasons of the year mark the changes of energy on our planet, which is demonstrated by the migration of animals as well as the growth and decline of plants and all they bear.

Participation in the seasonal rites places the Witch in the direct flow of energy, which is drawn and accumulated in ritual circles. Here the Witch is bathed in the condensed energy evoked within the magic circle, and the aura of the individual is charged with this power. Through continual immersion in the flow of seasonal energy, the Witch becomes more aligned with both the energy and the source of that energy. Therefore the Witch becomes more like Nature and the forces behind Nature.

The Witch observes the changing of seasons, noting the periods of gain and decline, and valuing this ever-repeating cycle within Nature. Here can be found comfort in knowing that loss and decline is not a permanent condition. Winter gives way to Spring, Spring to Summer, and Summer to Fall, each in its own time. The Witch understands that he or she is part of the cycles of Nature and equally embraces the attributes of each one. Therefore the Witch is rooted in balance.

A tree is rooted in the earth where it fixes itself in the world. Spring, Summer, Fall, and Winter encircle the tree, each one bringing changes to the life of the tree. Some people say that the tree endures Winter, but actually the tree endures each season. The tree is constant in what it is as a being throughout the year, and the seasons bring out only the tree's natural responses. The tree does not hate Winter or love Summer, it simply experiences them and lives in accord with the season. The tree is simply part of what is going on around it, and this is likewise true for the spirit of the Witch.

The lunar rituals in Witchcraft are designed to align the Witch with the energy of the moon in very much the same way as the seasonal rites. The waxing phases of the moon (running from new moon to full moon) are periods of gain when the energy is conducive to growth and creativity. The waning periods (running from just after the full moon until the time of the new moon) are periods of decline when the energy of the moon is conducive to decay and dissipation. Unlike the seasons of the year, the lunar energies present their entire cycle in the short span of one month. This makes the moon's energy ideal as a source of magic for Witches to access, but magic is only a very small part of Witchcraft.

The moon awakens the psychic senses in the Witch, which allows him or her to pierce the illusion of form and see into the inner mechanism. The Witch can gaze clearly into the dark hidden corners of the human psyche just as the full moon can light up the darkness of night. This is one of the reasons why the Witch was feared by those whose hearts were not true to their words and actions. Such individuals once sanctioned the killing of Witches, and there are still those today who likewise seek our demise. It appears that ignorance, intolerance, and fears are timeless traits.

In the next chapter we will seek out the Witch so that we may better understand his or her ancient spirit. How else can we get to know a people unless we learn something about them? Let us move on now and develop an informed opinion as we continue to examine the spirit of the Witch.

TWO

In Search of the Witch

There are many different images of a Witch. Some of these are based on facts while others are based on misunderstanding. Unfortunately some images and beliefs are based upon falsehood. Over the centuries Witches have been written about in myth, legend, fairy tale, and history. The Witch has been many things to many people, but can only be truly understood with the addition of an account by the Witches themselves.

Some people might be surprised to know that Witchcraft is both a religion and a spirituality. The majority of practices and beliefs found within Witchcraft are rooted in pre-Christian European religion. In addition we find, in modern Witchcraft, the inclusion of some mystical Eastern concepts originating in India and the Orient, but, as we shall see, there is no character known as the Devil or Satan in the religion of Witchcraft.

Writings about Witches occur in Western literature as early as the eighth century B.C.E. In the pre-Christian history of Europe there is no association or mention of Witches in connection with the Judeo-Christian entity known as Satan or the Devil. The concept of a personification of evil originated outside of Europe, and was later imported when trade with the Middle East and Egypt was developed.

The earliest literature to mention Witches in Western civilization appears in the ancient Aegean/Mediterranean region. Here early Witches were associated with various goddesses as evidenced in the ancient writings of Homer, Horace, Lucan, Ovid, and others. These goddesses were not "evil" in nature, and were popular among the lower or peasant class. This was particularly true in rural areas where the goddess Diana was highly venerated, and who appears in ancient literature as a goddess worshipped by Witches. The rustic peasant class was generally looked down upon by the middle- and upper-class peoples who typically dwelled in the cities.

The first deities/entities connected with Witches in early literature are primarily goddesses of the moon and of the Afterlife realm. In the earliest writings of Western culture concerning Witches, they appear as beautiful and seductive women. Two examples are Circe and Medea. The stereotype image of the Witch as an ugly old hag is one that evolves later over the course of many centuries. For the reader who is interested in knowing more about how this image arose from the purposeful maligning of Witches and the fostering of the distorted image of Witches, my previous book *The Witches' Craft* explores this theme in great detail.[1] Therefore I will only deal briefly here with this topic.

Prior to the transformation of the beautiful Witch image into an ugly hag figure, one of the foundational depictions of earlier witches is discovered in the ancient Greek figure of the *Graeae*. The name Graeae means "gray ones" and in mythology these three sisters are gray-haired from birth, symbolizing their wisdom and knowledge. Hesiod, in his *Theogony*, describes them "with fair faces and gray from birth, and these the gods who are immortal and men who walk on the earth call Graiai, the gray sisters, Pemphredo robed in beauty and Enyo robed in saffron. . . ."[2]

According to legend, the Graeae possessed great wisdom from birth and grew wiser as the ages pass. The Graeae were not originally referred to as Witches specifically, but such identification became the standard as their tales were retold in the future. In the retelling, the fair-faced Graeae of Hesiod's time become the ugly hags of a later period. One example is the depiction of the three Witches in Shakespeare's *Macbeth*, which is clearly based upon the distorted image of the Graeae of Greek mythology. However, as reflected in the prototypes of the beautiful Medea, Circe, and the fair-faced Graeae, it is clear that the origins of the Witch image are not rooted in ugliness but rather in beauty.

In the ancient Greek and Roman tales of such Witches as Medea and Circe, there is mention of praying to a goddess. Indeed, Medea is portrayed as a priestess of the goddess Hecate. The earliest written reference to Hecate appears in Hesiod's *Theogony*. Here Hecate is depicted as a great goddess favored by Zeus.[3] It isn't until centuries later that writers begin to portray Hecate as a dark goddess of the Underworld. Curiously as writers transform the nature and image of Hecate into something dark and foreboding, the image of the Witch is also negatively transformed in a parallel fashion during the same literary periods.

Ancient writings portray the Witch as living away from the towns and cities. Several ancient writers of the classical period portray Witches as living among the "herb-clad hills" and in isolated woodlands. This theme of the Witch living in natural settings, literally within Nature, is connected to the concept of Witchcraft as a Nature religion.

The earliest word used in Western literature to indicate a Witch is the Greek word *pharmakis*, which means a person possessing the knowledge of plants (particularly the drugs extracted from them). The modern English word pharmacist is derived from this Greek root word. The etymology strongly suggests that early Witches appear to have been essentially herbalists.

In later times the Latin word *saga* replaced pharmakis. Saga indicated a person who performed acts of divination or fortune-telling. The modern word sage is derived from the Latin word saga. The Romans replaced saga with the Latin word *venefica*, which originally indicated a person who prepared love potions. The meaning of the word venefica was later changed through an act of subterfuge, and became equated with poisoning. This is covered in detail in my previous book *The Witches' Craft*.[4]

One of the best ways to understand the truth about Witches is to examine those things that are consistently associated with them since ancient times. One of the familiar images of the Witch is a woman holding a broom, and standing before a cauldron with a blazing fire beneath it. Sometimes she is depicted as living in a cottage outside of the village, huddled before her hearth, whispering secret spells in the night. In some tales the Witch lives alone in a cave or deep inside a forest.

In the remaining course of this chapter we will examine these elements associated with the Witch, and we will uncover the truth that lies behind the prejudice and stereotypes surrounding Witches. In our quest we must look at the broom, cauldron, cave, tree, hearth, and fire.

Ancient writings (particularly among the Greeks) tell of a "divine" fire or "sacred" fire that burned at the center of the Universe before the world was formed. This fire was called the Vesta flame, which was pure and untouched by anything else. From this concept arose the association between virginity/chastity and the goddess Vesta.

In ancient times virginity and chastity were not automatically equated as being one and the same state of being. A chaste nature indicated that one did not engage in sexual activity with another. Originally a virginal state meant that one had never given birth. In the ancient cult of Vesta women were required to be chaste virgins. This was meant to symbolize the purity of outside independent power, something not requiring a relationship with another.

Fire was one of the earliest forms to represent divinity itself. Fire came from beneath the earth in the form of lava, and fell from the sky as lightning. Fire provided warmth, cooked meals, produced light, protected against wild animals, and transformed raw materials (clay into pottery, wood into ashes, and so forth).

In ancient Greek mythology fire was originally an exclusive possession of the gods. According to legend, the Greek hero Prometheus stole fire from Zeus (and in some tales, from the fire god Hephaestus) and concealed it in a bundle of fennel stalks. Prometheus then delivered the fire to humankind. In some northern European tales a bird captures fire and brings it to humankind. In these myths the bird is either a wren or a robin-redbreast. It is interesting to note that Prometheus is intimately linked to an eagle in this myth, which may be a remnant of an earlier tale in which the eagle retrieved fire from the gods.

Plato, in his work *Protagoras*, writes that the gods created all mortal creatures beneath the ground, making each body from earth and fire.[5] This mythos creates a connection between the Underworld and fire. As we noted earlier, fire came from beneath the ground and also from the sky. In these two realms fire possessed different forms: lava and lightning. On the earth it manifested as pure flame. Therefore, the essence of fire existed in the three worlds: the Overworld (heavens), the Middleworld (Earth) and the Underworld.

In time humans learned to evoke fire from wood by using what is commonly known as the fire-drill method. This technique requires placing a piece of wood flat on the ground. A stick is then sharpened on one end and its tip is placed against the other piece of wood. Both palms of the hand are pressed together with the sharpened stick firmly between them. Rapid movement of the hands then turns the stick quickly back and forth in a drilling motion. The heat resulting from the friction of the wood eventually causes a flame to burst forth from the wood on the ground.

James Frazer, in his book *Myths of the Origin of Fire*, states that in early primitive cultures the fire-drill technique was associated with the act of sexual intercourse. Frazer also refers to a primitive belief that fire could be elicited from the genitals of a woman, and that early myths sometimes represented women as possessing fire before men. Frazer writes of an interesting connection between fire and women:

> For the fire which is extracted from the board by the revolution of the drill is naturally interpreted by the savage as existing in the board before its extraction by the drill, or, in mythical language, as inherent in the female before it's drawn out by the male; just as the savage imagines fire to be stored up in all the trees from whose wood he elicits it by friction. Thus to the primitive thought it might seem natural to conclude that fire was owned by women before it came into the possession of men.[6]

Many of the elements associated with fire that we've encountered in this chapter are connected to trees. Birds nest in trees or take shelter in the branches. Humans use the wood of trees for fire. Trees are also connected to Underworld themes, and thus back to fire again. In time, when fire became "domesticated," it burned in the hearth where women tended it. This important theme will be further explored later in this chapter, but first we must examine the significance of the tree itself. In order to understand this, we must know something of the primitive view of the Underworld.

For our ancestors the Underworld was a place of great mystery. Life sprang forth from beneath the ground in the form of plants. To the primitive mind it must have also appeared that something beneath the ground produced such creatures as the snake, weasel, badger, and other animals that live in burrows.

Our ancient ancestors knew that a seed must be buried in the earth in order for a plant to grow. If the seed were kept in a pouch, it produced nothing. Therefore, to the primitive mind, the power to create a plant did not dwell in the seed but in the earth. There was seemingly something beneath the ground that generated life.

From a primitive perspective the sun and moon also arose from beneath the ground and returned there again each day/night. A belief arose that deep in the ground another world existed. This mysterious realm came to be called the Underworld. Trees, with their massive roots extending deep into the ground, were thought to penetrate into the Underworld.

It is common knowledge that our ancestors once worshipped or highly venerated trees. Some trees were believed to house various deities and spirits. Tales of holy trees abound in European lore, such as the oak, ash, hawthorn, rowan, birch, and many others. Sacred groves were established and dedicated to various gods and goddesses.

Trees were not only rooted in the Underworld, but their branches extended into the Overworld. Birds descended and landed on their branches. In ancient lore, birds were messengers of the gods. Some of the earliest carvings of deities are bird figures, later evolving into bird-headed humanoid figures. This prehistoric theme survived among the Egyptian deity forms, many of which have bird heads. The hawk-headed Horus and ibis-headed Thoth are but two examples.

In ancient times, the image of a tree served as both a doorway to the Underworld and a guardian of its entrance. A hollow at the base of the trunk would be seen as a doorway to the fairy realm or Otherworld.

The tree not only reached down into the Underworld and up to touch the Overworld, it also stood firmly in the Middleworld of humankind. Here was its trunk, and in many folktales a hollow at the base of the tree was a doorway into the fairy realm or the Otherworld. Branches were taken from the trees as staves, and later wands were carved for magical purposes.

In Aegean/Mediterranean lore, the "golden bough" allowed safe passage into the Underworld, and in northern European lore the "silver bough" allowed access to the fairy realm. The mythical Odin hung on a tree and obtained enlightenment and the ability to foretell the future through a runic system. European slain-god figures were bound to trees, and even the figure known as Jesus technically died on a tree as well. In some cultures the dead were wrapped in animal hides and placed in the high branches of trees. Trees also once served as a primitive gallows.

Trees stood as both doorways to the Underworld and as guardians to the entrance. One of the most classic doorways was the cave, which was often hidden in a forest or guarded by the ash, oak and/or thorn tree. Caves were used as burial sites in early times and were often marked with spiral designs. Some anthropologists, such as the late Marija Gimbutas, believe that the cave served as a womb symbol suggesting a belief in rebirth. The endless cycle of the sun and moon rising and setting in connection with the Underworld no doubt suggested the theme of birth, death, and rebirth.

In ancient times caves were also used for oracle, as evidenced by the cave at Delphi. It was an ancient belief that souls of the dead could provide information from the Underworld, since they were already in the next world to come. Sacred wells, viewed also as gateways to the Underworld, were likewise considered to be oracle in nature. The openings to sacred caves were often marked with piled stones. Wells were also marked with a wall of stones.

Stone was used extensively in ancient religious practices. The famous standing stones found on the British Isles are some examples. Stone slabs were used as ancient altars, and even in later times "head stones" were used to mark graves. Erich Neumann, in his classic work *The Great Mother*, addresses the importance of stones as representative of the mountain and cave, themselves symbols of the "Great Mother." Neumann states that rock and stone have the same significance as does "mountain and earth" in the worship of the Great Mother.[7]

The symbols of fire, wood, cave, and stone all come together in one place as the hearth. Old hearths were made of piled and mortared stone. The cave-like opening of the hearth housed the wood and fire. As a mantle, a stone slab was laid across the top of the hearth (see illustration, p. 19). Here women tended the sacred fire of hearth and home, a domesticated version of the old Vesta

To early religions, stones represented the mountain/earth concept, and caves served as enclosures or containment for fire.

fire. In ancient Rome, ancestral shrines were placed above the hearth as a living connection to those family members who dwelled in the Underworld. Here again we see the cave symbolism in the hearth as an entrance to the Underworld.

Anthropologist Alessandro Falassi, in his book *Folklore by the Fireside*, reveals an old custom wherein peasants returning from the fields at sunset gathered before the fireplace. In front of the hearth, fairy tales were told to the youngest children, containing various messages and morals important to a community. The older children were told stories about their family members and ancestors. From such tales the new generation gained a sense of identity and of their place within the community. Falassi writes that, as the evening continued, the family spoke of their religious beliefs and customs in order to preserve their traditions.[8]

In earlier periods the fireside hearth was the center of the home. The family and the fireplace belonged to the mother of the home and it was she who tended the fire. In the center of

The hearth, containing the fire, surrounds it with stones, bringing earth and fire together for the benefit of the household.

the fireplace sat the "fire stone," a fireproof slab over which the fire burned. The umbilical cords of the children were placed beneath the stone. Here we see a possible symbolic connection between the new generation and the past generation (the cords placed as a bridge between the world of the dead and the world of the living).

In the book *Una Casa Senza Porte* (*The House Without a Door*), anthropologists Claudia and Luigi Manciocco make an interesting connection between the Witch and the hearth. The book deals with a figure known as Befana, who is a gift-giver Witch in Italian folklore and is similar to the Santa Claus figure in the United States.[9] However, Befana has an esoteric nature unknown in her common folklore appearance.

The Mancioccos state that the Witch Befana is an ancestral spirit that comes through the hearth and binds the current generation to the past generation. The food offerings left near the hearth for Befana by the children reflect the ancient Pagan offerings given to spirits of the dead. Stockings hung on the hearth are symbols of the Fates who weave the lives of humankind on their spinning wheel. Befana leaves toys as a token of the continuing covenant between the new generation and the past one. She also leaves a piece of charcoal, a link to fire and the dark Underworld.

Instead of coal, the main substance of the hearth fire was the log, which was burned in the hearth. Traditionally this log was taken from the part of the tree that was closest to the roots. This reflects the relationship between fire and the tree meeting deep in the Underworld.

On the fireplace hung the symbols of the woman, the keeper of the hearth fire. The female symbols were the cauldron, the broom, and the fire itself. In ancient times certain women served as priestesses of Vesta, and were the keepers of the sacred flame. In *The Golden Bough*, James Frazer makes reference to the divine fire:

For the perpetual holy fires of the Aryans in Europe appear to have been commonly kindled and fed with oak-wood, and in Rome itself, not many miles from Nemi, the fuel of the vestal fire consisted of oaken sticks or logs as has been proven by a microscopic analysis of the charred embers of the vestal fire . . . if Diana was a queen of the woods in general, she was at Nemi a goddess of the oak in particular. In the first place, she bore the title of Vesta, and as such presided over a perpetual fire, which we have seen reason to believe was fed with oak-wood. But a goddess of fire is not far removed from a goddess of the fuel which burns in the fire; primitive thought perhaps drew no sharp line of distinction between the blaze and the wood that blazes.[10]

Here again we see the ancient connection between the log, fire, and the female spirit.

Another symbol of the female spirit is the cauldron, which in ancient times served to prepare food for the family. For centuries the cauldron has been associated with the hearth where it hung above the fire. However, it is also one of the symbols of the woman's inner mystery tradition, where the cauldron is viewed as the vessel of Transformation. Erich Neumann writes, in his book *The Great Mother*, of women and the cauldron:

> The vessel of Transformation—viewed as magical can only be effected by the woman because she herself, in her body that corresponds to the Great Goddess, is the cauldron of incarnation, birth, and rebirth. And that is why the magical cauldron or pot is always in the hands of the female mana figure, the priestess and later the witch.[11]

According to Neumann, the tending of fire was at the center of the female mysteries. In the ancient "roundhouse" of primitive human culture, women created tools and vessels. The so-called roundhouse was typical of Neolithic dwellings and the only entrance or exit was a hole in the center of the roof, with the tended fire directly beneath it (literally, the house without a door). This symbolism was later incorporated into the structure of the temple of the goddess Vesta. Neumann writes of this:

> But at the center of the mysteries over which the female group presided stood the guarding and tending of the fire. As in the house round about, female domination is symbolized in its center, the fireplace, the seat of warmth and food preparation, the "hearth," which is also the original altar. In ancient Rome this basic matriarchal element was most conspicuously preserved in the cult of Vesta and its round temple. This is the old round house or tent with a fireplace in the middle. Models of these prehistoric houses were found in the form of cinerary urns in the Roman period.[12]

The female mysteries were focused upon the theme of transformation. The fire and the vessels that transformed raw food into cooked food were some early symbols. Primitive pottery ovens appear shaped like pregnant bellies. Vessels for carrying water also appear in this womb-like configuration (many of which are painted with stripes that resemble the so-called "stretch marks" associated with pregnancy). Here we see the connection between material substance and water, and the womb that transforms substance into a child that is born in the spilling of water.

Many magical cauldrons appear in ancient myth and legend. The sun god Helios rode in a magical kettle that renewed his form each day. The god Dionysos was made whole again in a cauldron of transformation, as was the Greek hero Pelops. In northern European legends, the cauldron appears as a vessel of enlightenment and of life-renewing properties.

Since the cauldron has been associated with magic since ancient times, it is no surprise to find it in the hands of the Witch figure. Standing before her hearth, where the divine female flame dances upon the sacred log that guards the entrance to the Underworld, the Witch oversees the cauldron of transformation.

Historian Diane Purkiss, in her book *The Witch in History*, speaks of the cauldron as a symbol of women's control over food production, which could be seen as a threat to the men of the community. Purkiss notes that the cauldron is not only a cooking pot but also a womb symbol from which metaphorical children are born. This is the Witches' magic, the birthing of the unseen into the material world and the opening of doorways into the spirit realm.[13]

It is only natural that the bubbling cauldron should come to represent the transformative powers of the female. The legendary potions brewed in the Witches' cauldron are reflections of the woman's body fluids, which to primitive minds must have seemed magical. For example, blood flowing from a woman for days (menstruation) without causing death or physical decline. Another mystery was the production of milk from the breast, transforming one life-giving substance (blood) into another.

Neumann theorizes that to early humans "a universal symbolic formula" existed: woman=body=vessel=world. Through this concept, Nature is viewed as the Great Mother and women as microcosmic representations of this goddess (her principles being seen through metaphors associated with the body and bodily functions of women in general). In this view the womb is reflected in the cauldron (where transformation takes place) and the breasts become the chalice (where nourishment is consumed in the fullness of the residing liquid substance).

The assignment of the Witch as a priestess, her traditional tools associated with the ancient female mysteries and connection with the hearth strongly suggests the deep roots of the Witch figure in the antiquity of religious and spiritual concepts.

Another magical tool associated with the hearth and with the Witch is the broom. The Witch's broom symbolizes the branch of the sacred tree that was once considered to be a god or goddess. It is the tree rooted in the Underworld and stretching into the starry night. Traditionally the Witch's broom was made from a branch of an ash tree. The sweep was made from small dried birch twigs, which were fastened to the base of the handle with strips of willow bark.

In ancient lore the ash tree is associated with "the waters of life" and with the sea. The birch was said to have power over spirits, which in ancient times were believed to dwell in the air. The willow, with its branches turned back toward the ground, was believed to bind things to the earth. Therefore the Witch's broom was linked to earth, water, and air.

When considering the broom to be reflective of the sacred tree that housed deity, we must consider what deity ancient Witches worshipped. The earliest literary mention of a goddess associated with Witches is Hecate. The ancient Greek writer Hesiod, in the *Theogony*, wrote that Zeus granted the goddess Hecate "a portion of the earth, sea, and the starry heavens."[14] It is noteworthy here to recall the broom's link to Earth, Water, and Air.

These images and connections depict the Witch intimately linked to Hecate, sharing with the goddess a portion of those things allotted her by Zeus. The broom is in some regards a key to the three realms, allowing the Witch the gift of spiritual flight to the starry heavens where the moon silently awaits.

The ancient writers Horace and Lucan depict Witches as worshipping Hecate, Diana, and Proserpina. Horace also writes that Witches sing incantations from a book and thereby draw down the moon from the heavens. The moon has long been associated with Witches and with the female mysteries in general. Neumann notes:

. . . the favored spiritual symbol of the matriarchal sphere is the moon in its relation to the night and the Great Mother of the night sky. The moon, as the luminous aspect of the night, belongs to her; it is her fruit, her sublimation as light, as expression of her essential spirit.[15]

As we have seen within the symbolism detailed in this chapter, the Witch is connected to some of the most primary and essential aspects of sacredness and divinity as viewed by our ancient ancestors. The tools associated with Witchcraft are rooted in hearth and home. They also share connections with Nature and associated primitive religious themes. They are also the symbols of feminine power and influence, both in secrecy and in open community. This topic is explored further in chapter seven.

In this current chapter we have explored the ancient roots of the Witch, and in doing so some of the misconceptions about Witches have been dispelled. It is time then to look at the religion that Witches practice. In doing so even more misinformation can be corrected regarding what Witches actually practice and believe. Let us turn now to the next chapter and continue our quest.

THREE

Witchcraft as a Religion

J ust as the nature, image, and character of the Witch has been intentionally distorted over the centuries, so too has the religion of Witchcraft. Some people believe that the rites of Witchcraft involve animal or even human sacrifice. Others believe that the rituals of Witchcraft are designed to worship the Judeo-Christian figure known as Satan, or the Devil. However, as demonstrated in chapter two, Witchcraft originated in pre-Christian Europe long before the concept of such a character was encountered in this region. Therefore its foundation is not based upon Judeo-Christian theology, which is essentially a foreign import originally rooted in Hebrew culture.

As mentioned in chapter two, the earliest writings associate Witches with various goddesses and depict Witches as living amidst the herb-clad hills outside of towns and cities. Ancient writings refer to them as the *pharmakeutes* (the herbalists) and as priestesses of such goddesses as Hecate.

Witchcraft has evolved over the centuries, just as many religions have. In modern times the religion of Witchcraft is one of the veneration of the earth and its life force, which we call Nature. Essentially, Nature is viewed as the spirit or soul of the earth. Witches believe that the earth is a conscious being, referred to as the Great Mother by some, and Gaia by others. From her all things are born, and to her all things return at the end of their time.

Most Witches (but certainly not all) conceive of a male consort figure associated with the Goddess. He is, in essence, the ancient Sky Father image. Some Witches perceive of deity as strictly a Goddess figure who has within her a gender polarity of masculine and feminine aspects. In such a view the God is an aspect of the Goddess.

Within Nature we find the ever-present concept of male and female, which is essential to the creation of offspring and future generations. Witches believe that divinity dwells within Nature, and that Nature is a diminished reflection of a higher divine reality. This belief is encapsulated in the adage "As above, so below," meaning that the lower dimensions/inner dimensions reflect the higher/outer dimensions. The reflection of the higher image is distorted or diminished in clarity within the material realm, much like a blurred or overexposed photo might be discerned.

The majority of Witches view divinity as being comprised of both male and female polarities, which they personify as "Goddess" and "God." The "Source of All Things" is considered to be essentially unknowable to the human intellect. To simplify it for human understanding, Witches personify the two aspects of the Divine Source. Therefore the Goddess and the God are the images of the creators of the Universe. The Goddess is the vehicle through which manifestation takes place and the God is the catalyst by which the womb of the Goddess is pregnant with the seed of creation. This is covered in more detail in chapter ten.

As one might expect when speaking of gods and goddesses, in Witchcraft we find many myths and legends. These tales are mixed into the theology of Witchcraft because of the powerful metaphors that they convey. The eight ritual ceremonies that comprise the celebrations in Witchcraft (along with the monthly full moon rites) are based upon seasonal themes and the myths that express them.

Because Witchcraft is a Nature religion, its rituals are aligned with seasonal phenomena as well as the course of the sun and the phases of the moon. Unlike ancient Witches, modern practitioners no longer believe the sun and moon to be deities. Instead modern Witches view them as signifiers and metaphors intimately related to life, death, and the journey of the soul (as well as symbols of the Goddess and the God).

In the following sections of this chapter we will explore several of the key elements of Witchcraft as a religion. Each of these is examined in greater detail in other chapters. However I feel it is important for the reader to gain a general overview early in the book. I believe this will make it easier for the reader to understand the concepts that wait in other chapters.

The Religious Celebrations

The beliefs and practices of Witchcraft are rooted in ancient fertility concepts associated with the seasons and with agricultural needs. The equinox and solstice periods mark the seasons of growth and decline within Nature. Therefore, at these times Witches gather to celebrate the forces of this endless cycle of life, death, and renewal.

The Witches' year is measured out in eight portions or divisions comprised of four quarter festivals and four cross-quarter festivals. The times that mark the exact midpoint between the equinox and solstice periods are called the cross-quarters. The cross-quarters fall in the months of February, May, August, and

October. Together the eight celebrations, also known as the Sabbats, are referred to as the Wheel of the Year.

In the popular modern Celtic-based traditions of Witchcraft, the Sabbats are divided into the categories of the "lesser" and "greater" Sabbats. Here the crossquarters are the Great Sabbats, bearing the names Imbolc, Beltane, Lughnasadh, and Samhain. The Lesser Sabbats appearing in March, June, September, and December bear the names Ostara, Litha, Mabon, and Yule. Let us look at each of these Sabbats.

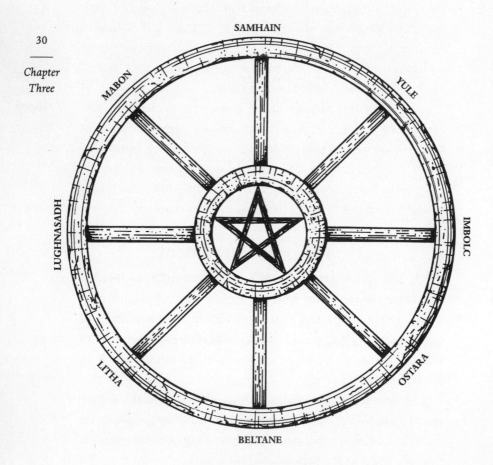

The Wheel of the Year

Samhain

Samhain is the beginning of the Witches' year. Just as a fetus comes to life in the darkness of the womb, so too does the "New Year" begin in this darkening season that leads into winter. This period is often called the Time of Shadows when, according to old traditions, the veil between the material world and the spirit world grows thin.

In Witchlore the so-called doorway to and from the Otherworld opens at the end of October and the past merges with the present. One of the primary themes in Witchcraft, which is commonly associated with this season, is the return of the dead from the spirit realm. This is not viewed as a negative thing, for these are the same people who we knew and loved in this life.

The meeting between spirits and "the living" is central to Samhain in the practices and beliefs of modern Witchcraft. Rituals and celebrations focus on reunion with those who have gone before. During this season spirits cross back into the material world, and the living reach over into the spirit realm and embrace the ancestral consciousness. Traditionally, offerings of food are placed to honor the dead through a feast of remembrance. Beans, particularly fava beans, were time-honored offerings to the dead.

The belief that one's ancestors live on as spirits is a very ancient concept. Ancestral shrines were often oriented to the east or west quarter, the region in which the sun and moon rise from the Underworld and set again, returning each day in an endless cycle. Offerings were placed on the shrines in order to maintain peace between the living and the dead. In modern times (as part of popular culture) sending flowers to the family of the departed has replaced the ancient act of laying out offerings. The traditional meal held at the wake has replaced the offering of food once made to the dead in ancient times.

As Samhain relates to the Otherworld, it also connects to the myths that are found in Witchcraft. The myths associated with

Samhain relate to the theme of the God and Goddess in the Underworld. This is covered in detail in chapter eleven.

Yule

Yule marks the day of the Winter Solstice, which is a sacred season that is venerated in the religion of Witchcraft. In essence, Yule symbolizes the renewing cycles of life, as well as rebirth, rejuvenation, and growth. In ancient Pagan times the Winter Solstice was the time when people believed the new sun god of the year was born.

As noted in chapter two, trees were considered to be sacred because the gods often dwelled within a tree. It was once the Yule custom to decorate the sacred tree in the forest in order to honor the sun god. An evergreen tree was selected because it symbolized the power of life to survive the seasons of the year. After decorating the tree with ribbons and other items, offerings to the sun god were placed before the great tree.

A time-honored Yule tradition still practiced by Witches today centers around the Yule log. The Yule log is traditionally a sacred oak or evergreen pine log used to call for the return of the sun's warmth and light on the Winter Solstice. The tradition itself evolved from the ancient fire festival of the Winter Solstice once celebrated throughout Europe. Some commentators believe that due to the inclement weather of the season, the Yule log ceremony was eventually moved indoors instead of being held in the open air.

With the rise of Christianity, the log was renamed the Christmas Yule Log. In the fourth century C.E., Pope Julius I designated the Christmas celebration to fall around the Winter Solstice. The Yule log tradition continued, but the fire came to represent the light of Jesus Christ instead of the light of the Sun. However, its origin actually arises from the ritual known as Yuletide, a pagan festival of fire. This is evidenced by the many quaint superstitions attached to the Yule log customs, which have no apparent connection with Christianity.

On the eve of the Winter Solstice, tradition called for the burning of the Yule log to usher in the power of the sun. The ashes were saved to disperse over the plowed fields in Spring. As part of the Yule tradition, a piece of the log was saved and used to start the fire for the next year's log. Dried holly was placed under the log to help kindle the new fire. The people gathered around the fire would toss in a sprig of holly, symbolizing the troubles of the past year. This act was designed to remove the old connections of the passing year and to purify the coming year.

In modern times, instead of burning the Yule log, holes may be drilled in a smaller piece of wood or branch to fit one or more candles, which are lighted for ritual use. The lights of the candles symbolize the waxing forces of Nature. For Witches, the light of the Yule log represents the Child of Promise, a mythical figure linked to the rebirth of the sun and symbolic of the coming year (see chapter ten).

As part of the seasonal celebration, some Witches place three candles on the Yule log to symbolize the principle of manifestation. Lighting the Yule candles and reciting a chant is a simple spell to attract prosperity and abundance. Placing a green candle (a symbol of growth and gain) can further enhance this by setting one in the holes at each end, along with a single red candle (vitality and power) placed in the center spot.

The first candle is lighted (and allowed to burn a few minutes each day) fourteen days prior to the Winter Solstice, and the second candle seven days later. The center candle is lighted on the morning of the Winter Solstice. Then all three candles are allowed to burn down together.

Imbolc

Imbolc is a ritual that falls at the beginning of February, marking the midway point between the Winter Solstice and the Spring Equinox. In ancient Rome, February was a period of passage signaling the end of the old year and the prelude of the birth of the New Year.

February was sacred to the Roman goddess Februa and her consort Februus, who were deities of purification and death. This festival season of purification was spread by the Romans into the Celtic lands where it later came to be known as Imbolc. In February the focus was on expiation of the souls of the dead, as well as personal spiritual and physical purification. The latter concerns were incorporated into a curious festival known as Lupercalia, overseen by a class of priests known as the *Luperci*.

During the Lupercalia celebration, the rites of purification and symbolic fertility were interwoven. The Luperci took strips of goat skin and began an unrestrained race in the nude, from the legendary grotto where Romulus and Remus were suckled by a wolf, along the via Sacra. During the race they would lay the lash across the backs or buttocks of any women they encountered in passing, thus assuring them fertility.

With the rise to power of Christianity in the Roman Empire, many pagan festivals were forbidden. In time Christian elements were grafted onto Pagan practices as one of many techniques used to convert Pagans to Christianity. Over the course of many centuries the old Pagan rites were continually modified until the Pagan vestiges were almost unrecognizable.

In the seventh century, the Roman Church adopted an older Christian celebration known as the Festival of St. Simon, and renamed it "The Presentation to the Lord." The date was changed to February 2 in hopes of permanently displacing the rival Pagan celebrations. By providing a conflicting time of worship, the Church ensured the presence of common folk who would not want to be counted absent from the Christian celebration, nor discovered as preferring the Pagan celebration, for fear of the resulting retribution by the Church.

The church festivals were successfully aligned with the month of February, a period once dedicated to purification in Roman paganism. By removing all the Pagan celebrations of Iunio Februata, the ritual of the Lupercalia, and the P{agan presence of the goddess Juno, February 2 became the festival of the Purification of the Blessed Virgin. In time it was changed to Candelora or Candlemas, so named because candles distributed to the faithful by the Church blessed the people. These candles were believed to possess protective virtues against calamities, storms, and the agony of death.

In a text known as the *Lunario Toscana* written in 1805, we read:

> In the morning, one does the blessing of the candles that are distributed to the faithful, which function was instituted by the Church to take away an ancient custom of the faithful that on this day, in honor of the false Goddess Februa, they went running through the city with lit torches, changing that superstition into Christian religion and piety.[1]

The Goddess Februa was evidently Iunius Februata, who was also called Iunio Sospita, the Savior. At the Calends of February, one celebrated the dedication of her temple on the Palatine Hill with a procession of torches. By the seventh century Rome created a Christian festival of nighttime processions with lighted candles from every parish, intended as a penitential procession to exorcise a resurgent licentious and carnal Pagan parade. The complete conversion of Pagans to Christianity was a slow and methodical process spanning many centuries.

The blessing of the candles took place just before the procession. Each candle was ceremonially lit from a main central candle. The ancient ceremony of the lighting of the candles had two meanings. First, it was connected to the idea of a universal religion (a Catholicism) apparent in the liturgy of the Church. Second, the candle flames symbolized the vitality of the evangelical teachings spreading out into the world, for such was reportedly the command of Jesus to his disciples.

In modern Witchcraft the flickering flames of the candles at Imbolc are linked esoterically to the leather straps brandished by the ancient Luperci. The central candle from which all others are lit is the life spirit of Nature herself, the fertile essence. Fire was a symbol of the divine energy of the cosmos according to ancient conceptions.

On March 1 the perpetual fire of Vesta was extinguished and then relighted as new leaves within the sacred temple were substituted for the old laurel leaves. The Vestal Virgins tended the fire, and when it was extinguished for whatever reason, the new flame could not be lit from another hearth. The fire had to be new, obtained by the friction of boring/drilling a piece of wood taken from a fruit-bearing tree. In this we see the connection of the old wood of the last season replaced by the wood of the new season, a metaphor of death and rebirth.

The connection of the dead and themes of death within the Roman celebration of February never disappeared, even in the faraway conquered territories of the Roman Empire, for the full moon following this month begins the time of self-purification known as Lent. This is a remnant of the old rites of February, which heralded the coming season of renewal. In observances of Lent we see a giving up or dying away of the old nature as Spring embraces the land.

Ostara

Ostara (Spring Equinox) is the season of celebrating the return of Spring. In the mythology of Witchcraft the goddess returns from the Underworld at this time. Witches therefore welcome the return of the Goddess back into the world of light. This, of course, is a metaphor for celebrating the return of the life force in Nature, which will bring new life back to the world following Winter's reign.

Beneath the soil long held in the embrace of Winter, the seeds of new life begin to awaken. In ancient times the first signs of budding trees announced the coming arrival of the Goddess. Ritual fires burned to encourage the sun to warm the soil and stir the sleeping life beneath it. Dancers came together upon the ancient sites to celebrate the Goddess and the promise of abundance symbolized by bud, leaf, and stem.

Traditional symbols of Spring celebrations include colored eggs, colored ribbons, budding flowers, baby rabbits, and newborn chicks. The egg is of particular interest because of its great antiquity as a symbol. In the Orphic Mysteries of Greece, the Great Goddess couples with the World-Snake Ophion and produces the Orphic world-egg from which all things originate. The egg of a hen later replaced this serpent egg when the Orphics adopted Apollo (whose sacred bird was the rooster) as their god figure. The Druids later incorporated this theme into their mysteries where we find the red egg of the sea serpent called *glain*.

In March the Vernal Equinox marks the first day of Spring. Modern Witches and Pagans associate the Goddess Ostara with this special season. A form of this goddess name appears in such early Christian works as the *De Temporum Ratione*, under the title Eostre (Ostre), who was the Anglo-Saxon goddess of Spring. In this text we find a connection between the German word *Ostern*, denoting an eastern orientation, and the word Easter.[2] Thus the related Goddess Ostre (Ostara) can be seen as a goddess of the East and therefore of the dawn. Modern Easter celebrations include a sunrise ceremony symbolic of the resurrection from death symbolized by the dawn. As the goddess of the East, Eostre was worshipped at this quarter of rebirth as the maiden aspect of Triformis, the Three-fold Goddess.

Traditionally, offerings of cakes and colored eggs were made to Eostre at the time of the Vernal Equinox. The symbolism of the egg as a representation of the seed of life is a very ancient association. Both eggs and rabbits are fertility symbols found in the ancient worship of Eostre. The rabbit/hare was sacred to the goddess of Spring and is still one of the focus points of Spring today found in the figure of the Easter Bunny.

The egg is an interesting symbol of great antiquity. The earliest icons of deities found in Old Europe during the Neolithic period are largely bird goddesses believed to have the power over birth and rebirth. To find the inclusion of eggs in the worship of Spring goddesses strongly suggests something inherited from long-forgotten fertility cults.

In southern Europe we find the Goddess Eostre under the name Eos, the Greek goddess of the Dawn. In ancient Rome it was the practice to carry eggs in a sacred procession to the Temple of Demeter. In modern times Italians still observe this in street processions during the *Pasqua dell'Uovo* (Easter of the Egg) where eggs are exchanged as symbols of spiritual rebirth. In Naples a traditional tart called *Pastiera* is made from wheat berries soaked in spiced milk and flavored with lemon and orange. This tart is descended from a traditional sweet made of tender grains sacred to Demeter. Another traditional food associated with Spring is the Italian *Pane di Pasqua*, the bread of Easter.

Myths associated with the Spring Equinox all reflect themes of the Mystery of Renewal. This is another reason why we see the egg appear in Spring symbolism. Marija Gimbutas, in her book *The Goddesses and Gods of Old Europe*, tells us that the ancient Neolithic Bird Goddess is inseparable from the Snake Goddess of this same period.[3] In Neolithic art the two goddesses are often unified as a single divinity. It is interesting to note that the Caduceus portrays two serpents entwined around a rod that bears wings (the serpent and the bird symbols). The Caduceus was the wand of Aesculapius, who was the son of Apollo. Apollo, as noted here, was associated with the rooster, and by extension with the egg.

With the approach of Spring comes the arrival of many birds returning from their Winter migration. In Neolithic art we find the Bird Goddess particularly associated with water fowl. The Snake Goddess is also associated with water snakes. Both goddesses appear with the ancient symbol of the V typically marked upon their breasts. This is the Neolithic symbol largely used to symbolize rain. Spring is traditionally a rainy season and it is easy to see the connection here between the goddess and her water symbol. Many ancient goddess figures, found in what is now Greece, depict goddesses bearing the V symbol.

Another symbol associated with the Bird Goddess is the labyrinth. The labyrinth is a classic Greek mythos found in such legends as that of the Minotaur. Gimbutas calls the prehistoric Bird Goddess the Minotaur's Mistress. Panels of labyrinth designs appear on anthropomorphic vases and figurines connected to rituals or festivals dedicated to water divinity. Perhaps the traditional Easter egg hunt is the memory of an ancient theme of passing through the labyrinth to retrieve the divine egg of the Bird Serpent Goddess.

Beltane

Beltane is a celebration announcing the coming of summer, and its ritual is traditionally held on May 1. In ancient times Beltane (also known later as Garland Day) commenced about eleven days later, prior to the change of the calendar. Therefore blossoms were more abundant, and hawthorn blossoms were available to be carried in May Day garlands (today this is not typically the case).

Beltane, by this name, is an ancient Celtic celebration of the return of life and fertility to a world that has passed through the Winter season. It is the third of the four great Celtic fire festivals of the year: Beltane, Imbolc, Lughnasahd, and Samhain. Along with its counterpart of Samhain, Beltane divided the Celtic year into its two primary seasons, Winter and Summer. Beltane marked the beginning of Summer's half and the pastoral growing season. The word Beltane literally means "bright fire," and refers to the bonfires lit during this season. It may or may not be derived from the worship of a sun god known as Belenus.

In ancient times Beltane heralded the approach of Summer and the promise of fullness. Herds of cattle were ritually driven between two bonfires as an act of purification and protection. This was believed to ensure their safety and fertility throughout the remainder of the year. The fires celebrated the warmth of the sun, its power to return life and fruitfulness to the soil.

Many modern Witches believe that the Beltane festival was held in honor of the god Bel. In some modern Traditions he is also known as Beli, Balar, Balor, or Belenus. Some commentators have suggested that Bel is the Brythonic Celt equivalent of the god Cernunnos.

In later periods the celebration of Beltane evolved into the May Day celebrations common throughout much of Europe. One popular May Day celebration is marked by the crowning of the May Queen who is attended by young girls bearing garlands. The garland is a symbol of the inner connections between all things, as well as a symbol of that which binds and connects. Garlands are typically made from plants and flowers that symbolize the season or event for which the garland is hung as a marker or indicator. In medieval times young men and women went into the woods at night, returning at daybreak with garlands of flowers or branches of trees. Great laxity was permitted to the maidens of the village on the night prior to May Day. In ancient Greek and Roman art, many goddesses carry garlands, particularly Flora, a flower goddess associated with May.

A Maypole is a tall pole garlanded with greenery or flowers and often hung with ribbons that are woven into complex patterns by a group of dancers. Such performances are the survivors of ancient dances around a living tree as part of spring rites designed to ensure fertility. The Maypole is often decorated with a garland as a symbol of fertility in anticipation of the coming Summer and harvest season. Tradition varies as to the type of wood used for the Maypole. In some accounts the wood is ash or birch, and in others it is the cypress or the elm.

The Maypole is traceable to a figure known as a *herms* (or *hermai*) that was placed at the crossroads throughout the Roman Empire. A herms is a pillar-like figure sporting the upper torso of a god or spirit. The herms is a symbol of fertility and often included an erect penis protruding from the pillar. The earliest herms were simply wooden columns upon which a ritual mask was hung. In time, to reduce replacement costs, the Romans began making the herms from stone instead of wood. In May, the herms was adorned with flowers and greenery, and sacred offerings were placed before it. This and other elements of ancient Italian Paganism were carried by the Romans throughout most of continental Europe and into the British Isles.

May Day celebrations can be traced back to the fertility rites of the Great Mother festivals of the Hellenistic period of Greco-Roman religion. The ancient festival of Floralia culminated on May 1 with offerings of flowers and garlands to the Roman goddesses Flora and Maia. The month of May is named for the Goddess Maia.

In the *Itinerarium*, written in 1724 by Dr. William Stuckely, the author describes a Maypole near Horn Castle, Lincolnshire, that reportedly stood on the site of a former Roman herms. The author records that boys "annually keep up the festival of the Floralia on May Day" and carried white willow wands covered with cowslips. Stuckely goes on to say that these wands are derived from the thyrsus wands once carried in the ancient Roman Bacchanal rites.[4]

The May festival incorporates elements of pre-Christian worship related to agricultural themes. In ancient times a young male was chosen to symbolize the spirit of the Plant Kingdom, known by such names as Jack-in-the-Green, Green George, and the Green Man. He walked in a procession through the villages symbolizing his return as Spring moves toward Summer. Typically a pretty young woman bearing the title "Queen of the May" led the procession. She was accompanied by a young man selected as the May King, typically symbolized by Jack-in-the-Green. The woman and man were also known as the May Bride and Bridegroom, bearing flowers and other symbols of fertility related to agriculture.

An old Cornish May custom was to decorate doors and porches with green boughs of sycamore and hawthorn. In Ireland it was once the custom to fasten a green bough against the home on the first of May to ensure an abundance of milk in the coming Summer. The ancient Druids are said to have herded cattle through an open fire on this day in a belief that such an act would keep the cattle from disease all year.

Modern Beltane celebrations differ from system to system, but most include various elements of pre-Christian themes. The Maypole is still featured in the majority of modern celebrations and assorted symbols of fertility such as colored eggs often appear as well. Female Witches in attendance often adorn their hair with flowers and wear medieval clothing at public festivals. The men often wear medieval-style clothing as well, and many carry a sword or a staff. In modern Witchcraft we find a blending of old and new ways, allowing for the growth and adaptation that will ensure the survival of Witchcraft for future generations.

Litha

Litha (the Summer Solstice) marks the longest day of the year. In northern European lore, the Summer Solstice marks the battle between the Oak King and Holly King, figures representing the waxing and waning forces of Nature. On the day of the Summer Solstice, the Holly King defeats his brother, the Oak King. Even though this is the longest day of the year, the days begin to grow shorter from this time forward.

In southern Europe, ritual battles were enacted by groups such as the Benandanti. Fennel and sorghum stalks were used as symbols of light and darkness in a battle over the fertility of crops and herds. In Italian Witchcraft the Summer Solstice is the celebration of the anticipation of plenty, the bounty of Nature, and the coming of the harvest season.

In many modern Celtic-based Traditions of Wicca/Witchcraft, the Summer Solstice festival is called *Litha*. The word Litha is derived from the Anglo-Saxon word *lida*, which means moon. Some commentators have suggested that *aerra lida* corresponded to the month of June in the Anglo-Saxon calendar, while *aeftera lida* corresponded to July. Some modern Celtic-oriented Wiccans believe that Litha was actually the ancient name of the Summer Solstice, although there is no historical evidence to confirm this. In the popular fictional work titled *The Return of the King* by J. R. R. Tolkien, the author uses the word *Lithe* to denote Midsummer's Day.[5] In modern Wicca the use of the word Litha for the name for the Summer Solstice first publicly appears in the late 1970s in such works as *The Spiral Dance* by Starhawk.[6]

Lughnasadh

Lughnasadh is traditionally a harvest festival celebrating the ripening of grain and the first fruits of the harvest. It is named after Lugh, one of the heroes appearing in early Irish literature.

He is almost certainly derived from the Gaulish god referred to by Julius Ceasar as the Celtic version of Mercury.

Lugh was the God of All Skills, the "Bright or Shining One." Funerary games incorporating athletic prowess were conducted in honor of Lugh during the festival. They were said to be in memory of Lugh's foster mother Tailtiu, who died while preparing the fields for planting.

Lughnasadh was also known as Lammas, from the Saxon word *Hlaf-mass*, the Feast of Bread. Festivities and rituals typically centered around the assurance of a bountiful harvest season and the celebration of the harvest cycle. Connected to Lammas was the gathering of bilberries, an ancient practice symbolizing the fruitfulness of the Lughnasadh rituals. If the bilberries were bountiful, it was a sign that there would likewise be a plentiful harvest.

Mabon

Mabon (the Autumn Equinox) marks the decline of Summer into the season of Fall. In the myths of Witchcraft this period is the time of the Descent of the Goddess into the Underworld. With Her departure we see the decline of Nature and the coming of Winter. This is a classic ancient Mythos seen in the Sumerian myth of Inanna and in the ancient Greek and Roman legends of Demeter and Persephone.

At the Autumn Equinox we also bid farewell to the Harvest Lord who was slain in the gathering of abundance. He is the Green Man seen as the Cycle of Nature in the Plant Kingdom. He is harvested and his seeds planted in the earth so that life may continue and be ever more abundant. This mythos is symbolic of the planted seed nourished beneath the soil and the ascending sprout that becomes the harvested plant by the time of the Autumn Equinox.

The Autumn Equinox officially marks the first day of Fall. Symbols celebrating this season include various types of gourds and melons. Stalks can be tied together symbolizing the Harvest Lord and then set in a circle of gourds. A besom can be constructed to symbolize the polarity of male and female, or simply to illustrate the Triformis Goddess. In the latter case the pole represents the fertile time of the Maiden. The binding that holds the broom straw represents the Mother who holds the family together and is bound to her children. The dried straw represents the Crone who keeps things in good order. As a symbol of god and goddess energy, the broomstick can represent the male principle as a phallus and the straw becomes the pubic triangle representative of the female principle. Through the use of such symbolism we maintain a connection to the ancient mysteries.

The Eleusinian Mysteries, originating in Greece, involve themes of descent and ascent, loss and regain, light and darkness, and the cycles of life and death. Rites associated with these Mysteries were performed at midnight during the Spring and Autumn Equinoxes. The Eleusinian Mysteries dealt with the abduction of Persephone by the Underworld God, a classic descent myth, and with the Quest for the return of the Goddess. Such rites were performed in honor of Ceres, an agricultural goddess who was patron of the Mysteries.

In the general mythos Persephone descends into the Underworld and encounters its Lord. Thus Life disappears with Her and the first Autumn/Winter befalls the earth. The Lord of the Underworld falls in love with Persephone and wants to keep Her in His realm. The gods intervene, pleading with the Underworld Lord to release Persephone. First He refuses because Persephone has eaten the seeds of the pomegranate, an ancient symbol of the male seed (as noted in the Wiccan Descent Legend; they loved and were One). Eventually He agrees, on the condition that She return again to His realm for half of each year.

Fall represents the life of the world waning away, symbolized by the death of plants. The Autumn Equinox is focused upon the departed spirit of the Harvest Lord and therefore upon plant sacrifice. Animal sacrifice evolved into plant sacrifice as the hunter-gatherer society became an agricultural society. The Harvest Lord is killed at the time of his ripened grain. He is known by many names, such as the Green Man, John-Barley-Corn, Haxey Hood, or Jack-in-the-Green. The ever-repeating theme of this concept speaks of renewal. This renewal is a refilling of divine energy back into the soil to replace what the crops have consumed. By consuming the Harvest Lord in the form of festival foods of the harvest, each individual came away with their own inner natures revitalized.

The Harvest Lord is often symbolized by a straw man whose sacrificial body is burned and its ashes scattered upon the earth. In agricultural societies the ashes were scattered over plowed fields to ensure the fertility of the soil. It is still an old European custom to burn effigies of mythical figures at the closing of one year. These remnants of Pagan worship displayed in agricultural themes are still seen in Europe today. The Harvest Queen, or Kern Baby, is one such example. In this tradition, the last sheaf of the harvest is bundled by the reapers who proclaim, "We have the Kern!" The sheaf is dressed in a white frock decorated with colorful ribbons depicting Spring, and then hung upon a pole (a phallic fertility symbol). This is the survival of the Corn Spirit or Corn Mother described by Frazer in *The Golden Bough*.[7]

In Scotland the last sheaf of the harvest is called the Maiden and must be cut by the youngest female in attendance. If the harvest is not completed by Samhain (Hallowmas), then the last sheaf is called *Cailleach*, or Old Woman. Just as the Kern Baby was hung upon a pole, the Cailleach (also known as *Kylack*) is traditionally hung in the barn. When the first grains have been ground into meal, a portion is placed in a barrel and mixed with ale and whiskey. Farmers are then invited to the Meal and Ale celebration where they all partake of their fill. Once in a thoroughly festive mood the farmers go into the barn and dance beneath the Kylack. This type of celebration is traceable to the ancient Roman harvest festival where celebrants danced beneath effigies of Ceres, the goddess of grain.

The Four Elements

Ancient myths speak of a time when chaos existed in the void, long before the world was formed. The gods then brought the four basic elements of creation together and set them in harmony. These elements are called Earth, Air, Fire, and Water. From a metaphysical perspective, everything is comprised of one or more of the four elements.

According to the mythos, the Divine Spirit bound the elements together in order to keep them in harmony and balance. Once stabilized in this way, the elements were overseen by Spirit. In Witchcraft this concept is symbolized by the pentagram. The pentagram depicts Earth, Air, Fire, and Water under the direction of the Divine Spirit.

The pentagram's points signify the elements: Earth, Air, Fire, and Water, directed by spirit.

Many Witches personify the elemental forces and assign symbolic mythological creatures to each one. The traditional order is: Earth (Gnomes), Air (Sylphs), Fire (Salamanders), and Water (Undines). Some Witches prefer to think of the elements as simply energy forces that animate Nature.

The element of Earth is the principle of solidification and balance. Air is the principle of expansion and dispersion. The element of Fire is the principle of transformation and vitalization. Water is the principle of mutability and purification. The binding principle or "fifth element" is Spirit, symbolizing the intervention or interaction of divinity.

By calling upon the elements, it is believed that the Witch can create something magical, whether it is an outcome, a situation, or the manifestation of a personal desire. In such a magical work, the Witch becomes "Spirit" over the four elements and directs and binds their energies for a specific purpose. This formula is the basis for many spells and magical rituals.

Ritual Tools

In Witchcraft there are four primary tools used in a ritual or magical context. These are the pentacle, wand, athame (dagger), and chalice. Each tool represents an elemental principle. The pentacle is a tool of Earth. The wand is assigned to Air. The athame is a tool of Fire, and the chalice represents the Water element. In some Witchcraft traditions the elemental nature of the wand is fire, and the athame represents air.

In effect, each ritual tool is a physical connection to a metaphysical concept and source of energy. The tools allow the Witch to align to each represented element and to achieve the necessary altered state of consciousness that makes it possible for the Witch to interface with the elemental forces.

Once connected with the elemental forces, the tools serve as vehicles through which the Witch can draw and direct the energy. Typical uses of the tools include casting a ritual or magical circle, casting spells, evoking/invoking deity, and summoning various spirits associated with Witchcraft.

Karma

Karma is the term of the belief that whatever acts a person performs (good or bad) result in an attachment to the soul of "cause and effect" energy. This energy influences the experiences the soul will then have as a result. As an example from a mundane perspective, if you decide not to take an umbrella with you out into the rain, this will influence the experiences you will have. If you hit someone out of anger, this will influence the future experiences you will have with him or her. Karma is the spiritual counterpart of the mundane laws of cause and effect.

Karma is not a force that rewards or punishes. It simply keeps one connected with the energy that one generates by his or her actions or lack thereof. This energy will link individuals together, not only in this life but in future lives to come. The energy link will continue until the reason for attachment is dissolved.

In order to dissolve a Karmic connection, one has to pay the Karmic debt, as it is called. Paying the debt involves either restitution or a changing of one's ways. This can manifest in many ways, including the offending person being placed in the same situation as the offended individual. One example might be that a thief in this life would experience great material losses in a future life, or a life that denies the person the acquisition of the things he or she desires in life.

In the case of the thief, the frustrations experienced in the next life provide the generation of energy that allows the karmic attachment to be "burned off" and therefore severed. Once freed of the debt, the soul can then move on to other opportunities for growth and evolution.

Reincarnation

It is an ancient concept that we, as material beings, possess a soul that lives after the death of our physical bodies. To our ancestors, the ever-repeating cycles of Nature as seen in the four seasons and the endless rising and setting of the sun and moon, all suggested the theme of renewal and return.

We know from ancient literary sources that certain Greek philosophers such as Pythagoras and Plato taught the concept of reincarnation, and that the Druids taught it to the Celts. By the time the concept appears in Western literature, it is a highly developed and complex tenet of belief. But its origins were, no doubt, rooted in a more primitive belief system from an earlier age.

Our ancestors knew that burying a seed in the ground brought about the return of the plant from which it came. Perhaps, to primitive reasoning, the same thing could be accomplished by burying the body of a loved one in the ground. The fact that genetics reproduce specific family features probably led to the belief that various individuals had returned again among those born into the family. Therefore a child whose nose looks like a deceased grandfather, or whose big toe is identical to a past great-uncle, might have made people conclude that an ancestor had returned. Such a theory does not negate the reality of reincarnation as a valid concept, but merely suggests a possible catalyst to the consideration of such a principle.

Today many people claim to recall past lives, and many occult (a Latin word meaning simply "secret") traditions teach techniques designed to help one remember previous lives. One of the values in recalling a past life is to better understand how Karma is influencing one's current life experience. However, even though Witches believe in reincarnation, most feel that the present life is where one should primarily focus his or her attention. The concept of reincarnation and its relationship to Witchcraft is covered in more detail in chapter nine.

FOUR

Becoming a Witch

In chapter three we explored the religion of Witchcraft and its basic tenets. In this chapter we will continue our exploration and look at how a person becomes a Witch. More importantly, however, we will discover what it means to be a Witch. In this journey many interesting things will be presented for your consideration. Let us begin with a few questions.

Have you always felt different from the majority of people around you? Does seeing the moon in the night sky call to something deep in your spirit? Are you naturally drawn to things of a mystical nature? When considering conventional religion, have you always felt there is "more to it" or that many things just simply do not make sense? Is your intuition often more reliable than your thought-out conclusions? Do you often regret not going with your "gut feelings" in a matter? If so, you may have something of the Witch inside you.

For centuries people have believed in certain signs indicating that someone was a Witch. Possessing an unusual birthmark, being born with a caul, or having two differently colored eyes was enough to declare someone a Witch. In old folklore, being born the seventh child of a seventh child was also believed to make that person a Witch. During the era of the Inquisition, the children of anyone convicted of practicing Witchcraft were likewise considered to be Witches. See chapter nine for additional information regarding the hereditary factor.

Within the community of modern Witches the debate rages as to how one becomes a Witch. Some people believe they are born Witches, others feel they have chosen the path later in life, while still others feel the path has chosen them. All of these views are reflections of the truth. Witchcraft is a personal spiritual path, and many people who come to the Craft feel they have returned home.

There are some people in the Craft who believe that a person must be born into a Witchcraft family in order to be a "real" Witch. There are individuals who believe that they have been Witches in a past life and have reincarnated once again as a Witch. Others feel they have always been a Witch, even though born into a non-Witch family. What then is a Witch, and what makes a person a Witch?

Being a Witch is, at the very core, a way of seeing the world and a way of believing and living in accord with that view. Being born into a Witch family does not necessarily mean that the person will live his or her life as a Witch (any more than being born Catholic will ensure the person grows up to practice Catholicism, or will even believe in its tenets). As in any religion or spiritual path, only a person who practices his or her faith and believes in the essential tenets can truly be said to "be" of that particular religious persuasion. Anything less than participation equates to little more than an association with that religion.

Simply reading books on Witchcraft, and basically agreeing with the general beliefs and practices will not make a person a Witch. Casting spells and doing an occasional ritual will also not make a person a Witch, nor will dressing "witchy" and decorating oneself with occult jewelry. Being a Witch is something much deeper and more intensely committed.

Charles Leland, a folklorist who studied Witches and Witchcraft in Italy during the nineteenth century, said that one could become a Witch by studying their lore and by keeping company with Witches. This suggests a focused and somewhat intimate degree of dedication and involvement. Authors (and Witches) Gerald Gardner and Doreen Valiente, in their mid-twentieth-century writings, spoke of Witches as the "hidden children of the Goddess" and as the "secret ones of the chosen few."

It is true that the religion of Witchcraft is not for everyone. Witches are typically very unique people, even though they come from all walks of life, educational backgrounds, and careers. One of the few common elements that all Witches share is a basically independent nature. Witches are not "followers" by nature, and they tend to think for themselves. They do not blindly adhere to religious tenets, nor do they place faith above reasoning.

There is a common expression used by many Witches: "Organizing Witches is like trying to herd cats." This addresses the core issue of the independent nature of the average Witch. However, it would be a mistake to believe that Witches cannot join together to fight for a common cause. Witches can and do come together in support of the Craft whenever the need arises. Witches are an important support to the Pagan community. The word Pagan is derived from the Latin *pagani*, which simply means a country dweller, as opposed to a city dweller. Later it was used to identify people who still believed in the old gods of field and forest as opposed to the solo God of the ancient Hebrews.

In the New Testament of the Bible, Pagans were often likened to goats in various scriptures, and the "faithful followers of God" were likened to sheep. Sheep follow a shepherd, and the old expression "Get one to go and they will all go" arose from the natural behavior of sheep. By taking advantage of this instinct, shepherds control sheep movement. Sheep tend to be timid, nervous, and easily frightened. Having little natural means of defense, they instinctively join together in a group called a flock. All members of the flock will follow any member of the flock that happens to lead.

The goat is a very different creature than the sheep. For the most part goats are very sociable, lively, inquisitive, and independent animals. Although independent, when in a mixed herd, goats prefer to surround themselves with others of their same breed. Goats have excellent night vision and are often active at night.

In goat herds the "queen" leads the group. This female usually achieves her rank by virtue of having the most descendants. The dominance of the mother over her young is maintained throughout life, and kids will prefer to remain nearby their mother, even if separated for years and later reintroduced.

The dominant male goat, known as a buck, is aggressive during the breeding season, but during the rest of the year is submissive to the queen.

Leadership over the herd is passed back and forth between the queen and the buck, based upon seasonal rule. In modern Witchcraft, women are primarily the facilitators and group leaders. In some Craft traditions, leadership of a coven is divided between High Priestess and High Priest, who each "rule" for a six-month period.

Women in the Craft tend to be strong, self-assured, and self-empowered individuals.

Men in the Craft are typically males who realize that the true measure of a man lies not in his ability to physically intimidate, nor in any demonstration of physical strength, but instead in knowing how and when to use self-restraint. Men in the Craft play a supportive role to the female leadership of groups and are protectors and companions.

In modern Witchcraft many Witches practice alone or on occasion with friends. This solitary path is not always desired, although some Witches do prefer not to be associated with groups. There are still areas of the United States, Europe, and other regions of the world in which people cling to the stereotypes of the evil Witch/Satanic Witch. This ignorance makes such people fearful and adversarial toward the Witch. However, Witchcraft is said to be the fastest growing religion in the United States and parts of Europe. Perhaps, in time, the adversaries of Witchcraft will take an open and honest look at the modern Craft.

Can I Ever Really Be a Witch?

As an author I receive mail from readers, and in many letters I see a repeating theme. People want to know whether they can become a Witch without being initiated by someone who is a Witch (and has a Witch lineage of his or her own). Many readers comment that people on the Internet discussion boards make them feel that without a teacher and outside guidance they can never be Witches. There is also the expressed concern that without a teacher the "secrets" of the Craft will remain hidden, which implies a deadend for those without access to the keys. See chapter five, the section subtitled "The Voice of the Wind," for some alternative views on this topic.

The argument that one needs an initiator presents us with the classic quandary: "Which came first, the chicken or the egg?" Did the first Witches somehow magically appear and then initiate those they deemed worthy? Or did certain individuals develop the qualities we associate with Witches, and then teach others how to obtain them as well? For the purposes of this book, the latter seems to be the most logical conclusion of the two scenarios. The last interesting question then becomes: Which group had the first Witches? Was it the teaching group of self-taught individuals, or was it the group that was taught by them, and therefore the first individuals to be formally initiated? See chapter five, section subtitled "The Witch as Priest(ess)" for more background.

If we look at the Witch as the answer, we must ask what he or she possesses that a non-Witch does not? If we accept that most Witches are not hereditary Witches, then we can (for the purpose of this discussion) remove the "something inherited in the blood" explanation. This leaves us with no genetic answer, which then rules out physical traits, ethnicity, and mutation (because Witches share no common visible similarities not also shared by non-Witches, and have no mysterious internal organs not found in non-Witches).

Why is someone drawn to being a Witch? We might ask the same question as to why someone is drawn to be a Christian, Buddhist, Moslem, Hindu, or a practitioner of Jewish religion? Since all of these religions are comprised of practitioners from different races and cultures, the answer again does not appear to reside in genetics. Perhaps the answer lies in the spiritual realm.

Stripped of our human components, we are left with the soul or spirit to examine. For the sake of simplicity, I'll use the term "soul" to indicate the consciousness that survives the death of the physical body. Is the nature of the soul different in comparison to the soul of a non-Witch before the soul comes to reside in a flesh body? Do souls come from different spiritual races and therefore possess different traits and qualities? These are interesting questions that I will leave you to ponder on your own.

According to oral tradition, humans bear within themselves the divine spark of their creators. This concept is explored in detail in chapter nine. Essentially the divine spark connects us to the source of our origins. It is a consciousness in and of itself. As sentient beings we share consciousness with the divine spark within us. This connection imparts to us many qualities and enhances others that we separately possess.

For the purpose of finding the answer to our question, we must look to one of our qualities known as potential. We do not arrive in the flesh as souls that possess all the answers. We do, however, possess the faculty of discernment, which can lead us to the answers we seek. Therefore we have the potential to discover whatever we devote our consciousness toward understanding. This unique quality of the soul can unlock the secrets we encounter when coupled with other traits we possess. This is something all souls share in common.

It has been argued that the soul provides our consciousness, and the brain is simply the mechanism for its expression in the physical dimension. Accepting this, I will use the term "mind" to indicate a cooperative venture between the physical brain and the spiritual consciousness. In other words, the mind is the manifestation of the consciousness that arises when the soul communicates through the function of the brain.

The human brain contains memory cells that retain information. All of our experiences are recorded in the brain's database. This includes everything we have ever seen, heard, touched, or thought about. This is essentially why we can recall passages from a book, lines from a movie, and so forth.

In order for us to remember anything, there must be a connection that brings up the memory. For example, if we are trying to remember the name of an actor, our mind is not going to find it in brain cells that retain the memory of what we had for dinner last night, although it might if the movie we were watching had something to do with the actor. In this example we might say to ourselves: "What was that actor's name . . . he plays in movies like the one I saw last night . . . yeah, I thought of him then . . . but I can't remember . . . hmmm, let's see . . . I was watching the movie and eating some rice when I thought . . . oh yeah, his name was _____!" This is what is commonly known as "memory-chain association." The brain was recording what you were doing and thinking about, and made connections between each bit of data generated during the experience.

It is the process of memory-chain association that lies behind the so-called moments of enlightenment we all experience. You have no doubt in the past read a passage from a book that made you say, "Oh, so that's why . . . ." Or you've said "Oh, so if this is like that, then that explains why. . . . " What has happened is that bits of isolated data in the brain's memory cells have suddenly formed a connection (chain-association) because of the new information. Therefore the connection between once isolated bits of data now form together into a new concept or level of understanding.

Once the connection is made, then the mind draws up the relationship and presents it to our consciousness. We then feel like we have understood something new. However, we already possessed all of the data and it was only the connections that were missing. In effect, we already *knew* it but had never *realized* it. We know a great many things because we are constantly recording data, even when we dream. The trick is to integrate what we know with what we understand, and this is what the Witch does.

The formula and the process already exist within you. You are a spiritual being in a human condition, and the necessary faculties to practice Witchcraft and to be a Witch reside within you. The only true practical difference between the Witch and the non-Witch lies in the achievement of understanding how to access and employ the inner mechanisms at will. Although much of this is guarded by the oaths of secrecy that most Witches honor, this was all once originally discovered by non-Witches who had a penchant for the quest of enlightenment.

In the beginning of this section the question was asked: "Can I ever really be a Witch?" In every respect, and in context with what I've presented in this section, the answer to the question is you. Only you can respond to the potential within you, and only you can allow others to rob you of your own free will. For as Witches themselves say, "Know thy seeking and yearning shall avail thee not unless thou knowest the mystery; that if that which thou seekest thou findest not within thee, then thou wilt never find it without thee."

The First Steps

Witchcraft is, at its core, a religion intimately connected with Nature, its inner mechanisms, and the seasonal shifts that affect the earth. It is common within most earth religions that the seeker spends some time in a natural setting. This is done in a conscious attempt to communicate with the spirit of Nature itself.

A camping trip, even for just a few days, can serve as an opportunity to be alone beneath the moon and stars. Here a version of the "vision quest" or "spirit quest" known from ancient societies can be performed. In such a setting the difficult questions are asked: "What do I believe in about divinity?" "What do I doubt?" "What don't I believe in?" Keeping a journal during this period will be useful in reflecting back upon the experience.

While spending some alone time in Nature, find a spot where you will not be disturbed for at least an hour. Take with you a bottle of water, some grains, some dried herbs, and eight small stones or pebbles. The herbs called vervain, wormwood, and rue are ideal for this purpose. You will need about an ounce of each herb. The stones can be of any variety, although quartz crystal is the most popular one to use.

Once you have found a spot where you can sit comfortably and undisturbed, place four of the stones to mark the four quarters of north, east, south, and west. Space them so enough room is left for you to sit in the center between the outlying stones. Then place one of the remaining four stones in between each of the four quarter stones. This will form a circle of eight stones around you.

Separate three-quarters of the herbs, grind them together, and then sprinkle the mixture along the circle of stones. Make sure the entire circle is lightly sprinkled with the herbs. Once this is accomplished, then sit directly in the center of the circle, facing east. Place the bottle of water in front of you, along with the remaining dried herbs and the grain. Use a small cloth on which to place the items.

Sit quietly for a few moments with the palms of your hands resting comfortably on the ground. Slowly take in a deep breath and slowly exhale. Repeat this three times. Next, bring your hands to rest in your lap and take note of the view in front of you. Study everything in your sight and be aware of the variety of objects all joined together here in the balance of Nature.

The next step is to become aware of you as a part of this setting. What you want to achieve is a feeling of belonging in the natural order, instead of being a "civilized visitor" from the world of humankind. This step is important, and you may have to ask for assistance from the spirits of this place. Although they do not communicate in language, as we understand it, spirits will understand the intent of what you convey in the emotional/heartfelt vibrations of your words. Therefore you must sincerely feel that you desire communication.

When you feel a sense of connection and are ready to proceed, pour a small offering of water on the ground, and say:

> Spirit of the earth, I am a seeker. Open now to me
> the old ways, and guide me in my path.

Next pour the herbs out on the ground in front of you, and say:

> Spirit of the woods and fields, I am a seeker. Open
> now to me the old ways, and guide me in my path.

The last step is to pour out the grain in front of you, and say:

> Spirits of life and growth, I am a seeker. Open now
> to me the old ways, and guide me in my path.

Conclude by speaking about your desire to explore Witchcraft, and ask to be guided. Once you have completed the process, give thanks to the spirits of the place. Leave the herbs and grains (these are offerings) and pour out the rest of the water. Pick up the eight stones and put them away in a pouch. Collect a small portion (about a palm full) of the herbs that were scattered around the circle. Also take three leaves from the area. Keep all of this together for use as discussed later in this chapter.

If you decide that you want to explore Witchcraft as a religion and spiritual path, then naturally you will first want to begin a serious study. I have provided a suggested reading list in the back of the book. The course of study may lead you to a decision as to whether or not you will want to dedicate yourself to the path. Traditionally, dedication is a period of personal commitment that spans a period of one year. During the period of dedication one lives in accord with the ways of Witchcraft. He or she also participates in "The Wheel of the Year," which means the eight Sabbats of the four seasons and the full moon periods.

A Course of Study

Prior to your year of dedication, there are several fields of study that you will need to investigate. A suggested reading list can be found in the back of this book. Naturally the first course of action is to read some books that will provide you with an overview of Witchcraft as a religion and spiritual path. In doing so you will quickly discover that there are many different perspectives to be found. This variety will allow you to find what resonates with your current needs and state of mind.

The second area for your focus will be upon the sense of deity in Witchcraft. It is important to understand the view most Witches hold concerning the Divine Source. Witchcraft, as a religion, falls within the general category of Paganism. To better understand this aspect we must dispel some of the erroneous preconceived notions connected to Paganism. In order to do this effectively, it is best to look at word origins. Knowing the origins of various words helps us understand what the people who produced such words meant by them in usage. To begin, let us look at the words Pagan and heathen.

In most modern dictionaries you will find the etymology of any word you wish to define. Etymology presents the root origins of a word as well as the changes and forms in the usage of any word. Knowing the etymology helps us discern the view that the originators of words had about the things that they labeled.

If you look up the word Pagan you will find its origin in the Latin word *paganus*, which meant "a country dweller" and from the Latin *pagus*, which indicated a person from a rural district. In later times Jews, Christians, and Moslems used the word Pagan to indicate someone who did not believe in their view of God. Some people also used the word Pagan to indicate a person who held no religious views, which has no basis in fact. Modern Witches use the word to indicate a person who believes in many gods and goddesses.

The roots of the word heathen are derived from the Middle English word *heth*, which refers to uncultivated land. Therefore a heathen was a person who lived away from the developed areas of towns and cities. In this regard heathen and Pagan bear essentially the same meaning. During the early Christian period the word heathen was used to indicate the "unconverted people." The Church also placed anyone it viewed as unenlightened and/or uncivilized in this same category. In modern times the word heathen has come to mean a person who does not acknowledge God as viewed by the Jewish, Christian, or Moslem religions.

The Witches' view of deity is rooted in pre-Christian gods and goddesses associated with the woodlands, the moon, the sun, and the realm that lies behind the world of the living. Therefore you will also want to study ancient mythical tales along with archaeological and anthropological studies on ancient deity worship. Your primary focus should be upon mother goddesses and goddesses of the moon and the Underworld. Regarding the gods, you will want to focus on sun gods, horned gods, Green Man figures, Harvest gods, and gods associated with death and rebirth in general.

Another area of study is pre-Christian festivals and celebrations. This will provide you with an understanding of what the ancient people felt was important in life. One of the interesting elements of ancient rites centers around fertility. When we look at the era of history in which these rites arose, it is evident from various writings that the earth was abundant with plants and animals. For example, birds were said to blacken the sky when they took flight because there were so many of them.

Despite the natural bounty in Nature, the ancient peoples still created rituals designed to draw abundance. This is because ancient humans lived in "common cause" with Nature, and understood that we must return something to the earth when we take something else. The rituals raised energy and directed it into the soil in order to return fertility. Offerings were given to the spirits of Nature to encourage their participation and assistance.

Studying the material outlined in this section and focusing on the areas recommended will help you come to an understanding of the essential core of the rituals of Witchcraft, the religious elements of the Craft, and the spirituality of Witches. If you find that the old ways call to you and resonate inside of you, then it will be time to consider entering into the stage of dedication.

Dedication

As previously mentioned, the period of dedication is a time of committing yourself to living life in the ways of Witchcraft. In most traditions the dedicant will acquire his or her ritual tools during this period. The year is broken down into elemental themes associated with each of the four elements. Each quarter of the year is associated with one of the four seasons, which themselves have an element assigned to them.

The season of Spring is linked to the element Air. Summer is represented by Fire, Fall by Earth, and Winter is tied to Water. Therefore, the ritual wand is acquired in Spring, the athame in Summer, the pentacle in Fall, and the chalice in Winter. Each tool can be ritually dedicated and blessed on the solstice or equinox that corresponds to the season.

Begin your period of dedication by setting up a small altar somewhere in your home. Your altar should include two altar candles, a goddess figure and god figure, an offering bowl, an incense holder for burning incense, and a vial of oil for anointing. The oil can be any scent that is pleasing and evokes a sense of Witchcraft when you smell it. Anoint yourself with the oil prior to any altar work you perform.

If privacy is an issue in your home, you can disassemble your altar when not in use. You can keep the items in a box that is secreted away, and you can even use the box itself as an altar. Ideally, however, it is best to keep the altar set up at all times. In this way the altar will begin to take on an atmosphere of its own as it accumulates the directed energies it receives from your attention. This is, in effect, its own aura.

As part of the experience you will gain during your period of dedication, weekly "devotions" should be performed. Monday is associated with the moon, and Sunday is associated with the sun. Therefore, on each Monday you will want to take a cloth and clean the goddess figure as an act of devotion. On each Sunday you will want to do the same for the god figure. As a special enhancement, you can anoint each statue with a unique oil, in other words a "goddess scent" and a "god scent" (see the section in this chapter titled "Selecting a Pantheon"). Any occult supply store or "Witch Shop" will carry a line of oils.

After cleaning and anointing each deity figure, light some incense and place an offering in your offering bowl. Generally speaking, flowers are good offerings to the goddess and seeds are good offerings for the god. Once you choose a specific set of deities, you will learn more about them and additional ideas for offerings will become apparent. In the beginning it is a good idea to conceive of deity as "The Goddess" and "The God" until you are drawn to specific ones.

In addition to weekly devotions you will want to at least perform an observation of the Sabbats, as well as the time of the full moon. Most people will start with working in a solitary setting until they are comfortable inviting others or joining with other practitioners. Traditionally a dedicant does not claim the title of "Witch" until completing the period of the dedication. The period of dedication itself commences with a formal ritual.

Dedication Ritual

A dedication ritual is essentially a formal act in which one declares his or her intention of becoming a Witch. You can create your own rite or use the one given in this section. Obviously you will want to read the rest of this book, along with several others, before you decide about whether to dedicate yourself to this path. Once you decide to dedicate, then you will commit yourself to a year of focused study and discernment.

The following simple rite of dedication is based upon an initiation ritual that reportedly dates from the fifteenth century. It has been modified for use in the public arena, and you can further modify it to fit your personal situation.

At midnight, when the moon is full, go out into an open field or a clearing within the woods. Take with you a vessel of water, another of wine, and a mixing bowl. Also take a small red bag containing a sprig of the herb rue as your amulet and a pinch of salt. Bring the pouch of stones and herbs with you that you used for your original spirit quest.

When you have found the right setting, pour some wine and water into the bowl and add the pinch of salt. Lay out a circle of the eight stones just as you did before. If practical, remove your clothing and kneel in the circle beneath the moon. Dip the sprig of rue into the bowl of liquid and anoint yourself with it, in the pattern of the pentacle: Forehead – right nipple – left shoulder – right shoulder – left nipple – forehead.

Then cup the sprig of rue in your palms and lift it up toward the moon, saying:

Hear me, O Goddess of the Moon,
Queen of all Witches,
for I bear the symbols of the Old Religion.
Hear me then,
and think yet even for a moment
upon this worshipper who kneels before you.

For I have heard the ancient call,
and I believe the words of the Wise Ones,
when they spoke of your beauty in the night sky,
when they bid seek and find you above all others.

Here as the full moon shines upon me,
receive me, O Goddess.
Receive me as your child.

Anoint yourself again with the rue dipped in the bowl, and say:

Goddess, beautiful Goddess,
Lady of the Moon and beyond,
Queen of all Witches,

Goddess of the dark night and of all Nature,
grant me your favor.

Anoint yourself a third time with the sprig of rue, saying:

In the name of the Goddess,
so may it be.

Gather up the items and place the rue back into the red bag.
Sit quietly beneath the full moon and listen to the sounds of the
night for awhile. When you feel it is time to leave, collect the
stones and put them in a pouch. Take the other items with you
and leave the area as clean as when you found it.

Once you have completed the dedication rite to the Goddess,
choose a day on which to perform a similar rite for the God. Select a wooded area that is not so thick with trees that it prevents
your view of the sun. Take with you a bowl, and a bottle of
water. At noon set out your circle of stones. Enter the circle and
sit in the center area.

Pour some water into the bowl and dip an acorn into the
bowl and anoint yourself with it, in the manner of the pentacle:
Forehead – right nipple – left shoulder – right shoulder – left nipple – forehead.

Then cup the acorn in your palms and lift it up toward the
sun, saying:

Hear me, O God of the Sun,
Lord of all Witches,
hear me for I bear the seed of Light.
Think yet even for a moment
upon this worshipper who kneels before you.

For I have heard the ancient call,
and I believe the words of the Wise Ones,
when they spoke of your power in the day sky,
when they did seek and find strength in you
above all others.

Here as the sun shines upon me,
receive me, O Lord,
Receive me as your child.

Anoint yourself again with the acorn dipped in the bowl, and say:

God, powerful God,
Lord of the Sun and beyond,
Lord of all Witches,
God of the light of day
and of all Nature,
grant me your favor.

Anoint yourself a third time with the acorn, saying:

In the name of the God,
so may it be.

Gather up the items and place the acorn in the pouch. Sit quietly beneath the sun and listen to the woodland sounds of the day for awhile. When you feel it is time to leave, collect the stones and put them in your pouch with the acorn. Take the other items with you and leave the area as clean as when you found it.

Selecting a Pantheon

Most Witches, at some point, will select a god and goddess form that resonates with them. Many Witches will seek a specific god and goddess from the mythology of their ancestors. Some Witches will be drawn to deities from the myths and legends appearing in a culture that has no direct bloodline connection to the seeker. Others will discover that a god and goddess have chosen them instead.

It is not essential that you search for your deities within your own nationality connections to the past. You can serve a god and goddess from any culture equally well. You can also practice a

Witchcraft Tradition from any culture that you feel drawn to. There is, however, a definite and specific flow of energy in connection with traditions associated with one's bloodlines. In the end, you will make the choice that is right for you. It is a choice that at a later time you can change in accord with your needs.

When choosing a Goddess and God, it is important to understand that this becomes a mated pair. Therefore make sure that the two deities are compatible. For example, mating a goddess of peace with a god of war would not be a good match. The unions of their energies when invoking or evoking them would be like trying to blend oil and water together.

In most cases, things will proceed better when you do not try to match deities from different cultures. For example, mating an Egyptian god with a Celtic goddess might create a certain disharmony. This is because every god and goddess was given form and character within a defined cultural understanding and expression. Therefore gods and goddesses from various lands have their own flavor or vibration. In addition, many deities already possess mates in their mythological and legendary tales. Here ancient wisdom might serve us better than modern creativity.

It is advisable to study the ancient tales and to note the friends, allies, mates, love interests, adversaries, and enemies of any deity you are considering to include in your pantheon. What you will readily discover, in most cases, is that although various deities had affairs with other gods and goddesses, these relationships did not last nor develop into anything long term. When choosing a mated Goddess and God figure for your pantheon, you might want to give consideration to the stability of the relationship itself.

In Witchcraft, as a religion, you will find certain basic and central themes associated with the deities of the Craft. This is covered in greater detail in chapter nine, so I will only briefly outline it here. The Goddess is intimately linked with the moon, and she has a triformis nature personified as Mother, Maiden, and Crone. She is also identified with the Great Goddess/Great Mother figure and with Nature as a personification.

The God is intimately linked with the sun, and he has a triformis nature personified as the Hooded One, the Horned One, and the Old One. He is also identified with the Great Father/Sky Father figure and with Nature as the personification of the impregnating principle.

Both the Goddess and the God in Witchcraft share the attributes of Underworld deities. The forces of light and darkness, life and death, growth and decline, are all present in the deity forms of Witchcraft. The principles of transformation, rejuvenation, renewal, regeneration, and rebirth are also reflected in the deities of Witchcraft.

When choosing deity forms for your altar and for your focus of worship and ritual practice, you will want to consider the basic elements listed in this section. Examine the myths and legends of any deity you are considering, and note the presence or absence of the traits listed here. This will help ensure the most practical mating of a God and Goddess for use in your pantheon.

Connecting with Deity Images

Some people, especially those from Judeo-Christian backgrounds, have difficulty with venerating deity through the representative images of a god and goddess statue. Some Witches also have difficulty when changing to a new pantheon, and feel awkward about using different images from those of their previous tradition. In reality any images, names, and attributes relating to Divinity are simply human constructions.

I have devised a simple ritual that can help when shifting from monotheism to polytheism, or when transitioning from one cultural Craft Tradition to another. It involves addressing one's former concept of deity and then renaming it and assigning it to a new form. To begin, select the God and Goddess images that you wish to work with and place them on an altar. Set a sky-blue-colored candle in the center of your altar, and light the candle.

How you begin to address divinity here will depend upon what you are transitioning away from or toward, depending upon your own views. You may wish to open by saying "God" or "Great Spirit" if shifting from monotheism to polytheism. You may wish to say "Lord and Lady" if you are simply changing pantheons.

When you are ready, look at the images on your altar and then say the following words:

> (God/Great Spirit/Lord and Lady), pardon three things that are due to my human condition:
>
> You have no form, and yet I give you these forms here on my altar (pass your hand in a sweeping gesture in front of the images).
>
> You have no name and yet I now call you (give deity names for each image as you hold your hand out, palm facing each statue, one at a time).
>
> You exist in all places and all times, and yet I venerate you here and now.

A modification of this technique can also be used when shifting from one patron deity to another. For example, if one had been a priest(ess) of Hecate for several years and now wants to work with the Goddess Diana, this technique would allow for a smooth transition.

Once you select a new Goddess image, you would then place the statue on your altar. With your eyes closed you would envision the form of Hecate. Next you would say:

> Hecate, pardon three things that are due to my human condition: You have many forms and yet I now venerate you in the form of the goddess

_____. I have called you by the name of Hecate and yet I now call you _____. You have many aspects and yet I now venerate you as the Goddess of _____.

With time, you will no doubt wish to modify these techniques to suit your personal views. Essentially the ritual of transition is for your own psyche, for the deities are well beyond the dispositions, restrictions, and limitations that our minds, hearts, and souls impose upon them.

Seeking Other Practitioners

It is likely that in time you will want to seek the companionship of like-minded individuals. There are several ways to go about this, and each has its good points and bad points. You will need to walk this journey with great care, discernment, common sense, and intuition.

Check your phone book for a local occult supply store or Witch Shop in your area. Such places can connect you with other people involved in the same pursuits. Most shops offer classes on various topics, and this allows you to expand your knowledge. It also increases the chances of meeting people that you might want to practice the Craft with. Trust your intuition and first impressions when meeting people in this way. Don't rush into anything, as there is no hurry. While the vast majority of Witches are good, safe, and ethical people, there are also some individuals who will misuse the Craft for personal gain, sex, political advantage, and ego gratification. Every religion has its "bad apples," and Witchcraft is unfortunately no exception.

In addition to seeking out a local shop or meeting place, obtain a copy of the local newspaper and check out community events. See if your community has a Learning Annex program, for many do and they offer introductory classes. Many bookstores carry magazines that can be helpful in your seeking of information and community resources.

Another source for meeting other like-minded people is the Internet. Many websites have chat rooms and forums that you can join in on. Unfortunately a small minority of people with bitter hearts and runaway egos frequent the vast majority of these places. Such behavior falls under the category of "flaming" and is typically discouraged or simply not tolerated by the moderators of the groups. Regretfully things occasionally flare up despite the best of intentions. See chapter twelve for some advice in dealing with difficult people.

White, Gray, and Black Witches

Witches do not typically place one another into categories. In fact, Witches often resist labels and definitions. If you spend any time among Witches, you will find little agreement on what actually constitutes a Witch, particularly when trying to sort out people who claim to be Witches from one another. Even though in the Craft community the politics of who is really a Witch and who is a "wanna-be" or a "poser" exists, it is still difficult to find widespread agreement as to the definition of an "authentic" Witch.

Many people have attempted to categorize Witches as white, gray, or black. For such people, white equates to good, black to evil, and gray to a middle ground between the two concepts. Since Witches do not believe in the concept of evil as a thing in and of itself, these categories are not typically ones that Witches use to identify themselves and each other.

Since many non-Witches use the terms white, gray, and black, we will examine the basic concepts in order to demonstrate the differences among those who call themselves Witches. A white Witch is essentially one who performs only positive works of magic and will not work against another for any reason. A gray Witch is one who blends both defensive and offensive magic into his or her Craft. Such a Witch will cast a binding spell to prevent another from performing harmful acts.

The so-called black Witch works magic for personal gain regardless of the consequences or the impact that may occur concerning other people. A black Witch is someone who would cast an offensive spell on an innocent person as readily as he or she would upon an enemy. Fortunately, the black Witch constitutes a very small portion of those who call themselves Witches.

Regretfully, all of this reflects human nature and is not unique to religion. People rob, injure, and murder each other every day in the streets of our cities. As we've seen in the news, executives of large corporations cheat, manipulate, and defraud people as a general course of business. Even some lawmakers and politicians are willing to violate or abuse the trust we all place in them. In many cases lying, deceiving, misdirecting, and fostering secret agendas have become simply "doing the business" of economics and politics. I believe that the numbers and actions of "bad apples" among Witches greatly pale in comparison.

Now that we have looked at some of the various aspects of becoming a Witch and being a Witch, there is still much to learn. In the next chapter we will examine the spirituality of the Witch in the mystical sense. Let us turn now to the moonlit night when the Witch calls to the starry heavens as the rays of the moon bathe the Witch in welcome.

FIVE

The Witch in Moonlight

In ancient writings we encounter the term *Night Witches*. Historian Richard Gordon, in his article "Imagining Greek and Roman Magic" (appearing in Ankarloo and Clark's *Witchcraft and Magic in Europe: Ancient Greece and Rome*) writes that the Night Witch was legendary as opposed to the type of Witch that a person might actually encounter. But, as Gordon admits, the "two refuse to remain distinct" in ancient literature. The Roman poets frequently portrayed the Witch as a composite figure: a root cutter, soothsayer, and sorceress.[1]

In this chapter we will explore the spirituality of the Witch. Here we will discover the inner world of the Witch, the night spirit that gazes upon the moon and sees into the Otherworld. In addition we will look into the essential "theology" of Witchcraft as a religion, and delve further into the independent and intuitive nature of the Witch.

Unlike many religions, the practitioners of Witchcraft do not typically erect temples or physical church buildings. To a Witch, Nature is the temple, and the church stretches as far as the eye can see to the horizon in all directions. The Witch sees the sacredness of creation manifested in the trees, rocks, mountains, streams, lakes, and oceans. He or she is the steward of Nature, a priestess or priest of the Old Ways wherein veneration was taught. The people of the Old Ways lived in common cause with Nature and did not seek to master Nature, but instead strove to live in harmony with the natural order of things.

The inner spiritual center of the Witch is all about alignment and integration. The spiritual quest of the Witch is to discover one's place and purpose in this world and the next. The Witch understands that both realms comprise the greater reality of what truly constitutes existence and its purpose. The material realm, and existence within it, is only part of the equation. Just as the conscious mind and the subconscious mind represent different aspects of ourselves, the material and spiritual realms are reflections of a greater truth that surrounds the soul.

To uncover this "greater truth," the Witch looks to the inner mechanisms of Nature. Believing that the gods created the worlds (being in effect the artists of creation) the Witch examines the material and spiritual realms for signs of the nature of the creators. For example, on a mundane level, a painting or a statue reveals a great deal about the artist. We can perceive something about his or her spirit and personality by looking at the composition, use of colors, and general "feel" of the work. Even the artist's passion, or lack thereof, is reflected in his or her art. So too does creation reflect the artists behind it.

The Witch does more than merely examine the inner mechanisms of Nature—he or she participates in the pattern. This is accomplished through rituals that mark the seasons of Nature. Other rituals mark the power and influence of the moon and the sun. The rituals are designed to bring one closer to the cycles of

Nature and to draw and condense the vital essence for the ritual participants to absorb. Bathing in such energy establishes a harmonious relationship between the energy of Nature and the auras of the ritualists. From a magical perspective, to be more like something is to draw one step closer to resonating as does the thing itself. Participating in a Nature ritual draws Witches closer to the source of Nature. Venerating Nature, and seeing within it the sacred spaces, draws the heart closer to a healthy relationship with the divinity within all things. For Witches, divinity is expressed as both a Goddess and a God (see chapter ten).

The Moon as a Spiritual Metaphor

Who has not looked at the full moon in the night sky and felt the beauty of its soft light? In modern times the full moon is often a setting for lovers, as though the moon itself emanated some unseen romantic force that drew hearts together. The moon has also caused poets to write beautiful and haunting verses to its mystery.

For Witches, the Goddess reveals things that are hidden in the dark corners of the human psyche. Just as the moon (her symbol) lights up the darkness of night, so too does the Goddess reveal what lies deep in the human heart. The moon is a powerful symbol of "enlightenment in the places of darkness." This is why the arrow or dart of the Goddess Diana was a symbol of the moonbeam. With it Diana could impart enlightenment or "lunacy" as She deemed appropriate. The dart of Diana, stylized as a dagger, frequently appears on an old Witches' charm made of silver and known as the *cimaruta* (pronounced chee-mah-roo-tah).

The symbols on the cimaruta charm declare the connections of the Witch to deity and the realms that lie beyond the physical dimension. The symbols on the cimaruta are (given here counterclockwise in appearance) the rooster, the dagger, the moon with coiled serpent, the key, and the vervain blossom. The

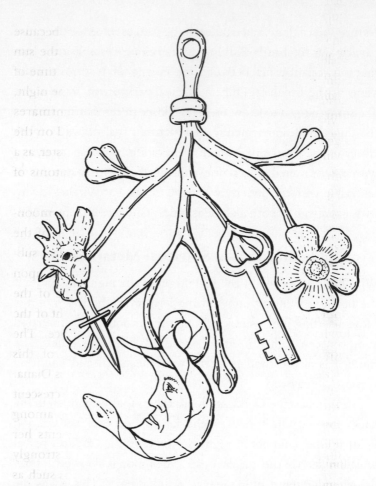

A Witch's charm, called a cimaruta, features images that have significance for the Witch.

framework design of the cimaruta is a sprig of the herb called rue.

The stem of the rue plant naturally divides into three branches, which links it with the triformis aspects of the goddess of Witchcraft. The rue amulet, as a simple sprig, appears in ancient Etruscan culture where it symbolized protection. On the cimaruta amulet, each charm appears as though it was a blossom on the stalk of the rue. Let us look at each symbol.

The rooster is sometimes called the herald of the sun because it crows in the morning. Our ancestors believed that the sun banished or drove away the darkness. The night was a time of danger for our ancestors. Predatory animals prowled the night, criminals performed their dastardly deeds, and nightmares plagued the dreamer. Therefore the sun (personified on the cimaruta as the rooster) became a savior figure. The rooster, as a charm, symbolizes the power to drive away the phantoms of darkness.

The dagger appearing on the cimaruta represents the moonbeam or ray of moonlight. Since ancient times the light of the moon has held the occult reputation of being a magical substance. In ancient times the reflection of the full moon upon such lakes as Nemi was considered to be the presence of the moon goddess herself. Through this connection, the light of the moon came to be identified with a spiritual essence. The cimaruta dagger symbolizes the directed movement of this essence, and as noted earlier is the arrow of the Goddess Diana.

It is no coincidence that the dagger points to the crescent moon on the cimaruta. Here the moon symbolizes, among other things, the bow of Diana. Therefore it represents her power or primal force. In ancient times the moon was strongly associated with Witches and Witchcraft. Roman poets such as Horace wrote that witches sang chants that could draw down the moon from the heavens. It was a popular belief in ancient times that Witches captured some of the moon's rays and kept them in a box, which was later used to add power to their magic.

The ancient vision of the moon centered on it rising from beneath the earth (for so it seemed) and sinking back into the earth when its journey across the sky was completed. In ancient times people believed that beneath the earth a great Underworld existed wherein the souls of the dead came to dwell. From this concept arose an association between the moon and the dead. A very old belief held that as souls departed from this world, the moon gathered them up. As the number of souls grew and were received by the moon, it became full. As souls reincarnated back into the world of the living, the moon's light ebbed away in accord.

The serpent on the cimaruta is featured coiled around the moon. Here it represents the Goddess Proserpina, the goddess of night and the Underworld. Although her name is the Roman form of the Greek Persephone, they are not identical goddesses. Ancient writers such as Lucan refer to Proserpina as the "last and lowest" of the three aspects of Hecate. Her name is derived from the Latin *serpere,* to creep or crawl, rendered *proserpere,* meaning to crawl forward.

Proserpina was identified with the moon and the serpent because both disappear into the earth and seemingly change shape in their overall movement. On the cimaruta, Proserpina is stylized as a serpent moving along the edge of a crescent moon. In ancient art Proserpina is often depicted astride a sea creature, and she holds its tail in her hand. The dolphin is associated with Proserpina—she is frequently shown riding it off toward the Underworld. On some forms of the cimaruta charm (varying from region to region), the fish symbolizes Proserpina.

The key appearing on the cimaruta is a symbol of the hidden mysteries and the power to open or bar them. The key is also associated with the goddess Hecate and is one of her symbols. In effect, the key represents the waning and waxing forces that turn the lock that fastens or frees the moon in each phase. The presence of the key also suggests one who possesses the key, the gatekeeper of the mysteries.

The last charm on the cimaruta is the vervain blossom. Vervain, in ancient plant lore, was an herb sacred to the Fay or Fairy race. In European folklore, the Fairy and the Witch often appear as kindred beings, and in some cases (such as the *donna di fuora* found in Sicilian lore), there is little if any difference between them. The Fairy, like the Witch figure, is also a keeper of the doorways between the worlds. In many Fairy legends doorways to the kingdom of the Fay lie in the hollow of trees or hidden in a mound of earth.

In ancient beliefs it was the Fairy who tended Nature, raised the sprout, vitalized the stalk, and opened the flower. The Fairy race operated the inner mechanism of Nature and guarded it against harmful intruders. The Witch and the Fairy established a covenant of stewardship and guardianship, with the Witch and the Fairy on opposite sides of the border of the "world between the worlds."

When we look upon the cimaruta as a composite image, we find that it speaks of the spirit of the Witch. In the rooster we see the Witch as one who dispels the phantoms of illusion. The dagger reveals that the Witch is a channel for the magical forces of the moon. The symbol of the moon displays the primal force that empowers the Witch. The serpent is a reminder of the Witch in connection with the realms that lie beyond the mundane world of humankind. In the key the Witch is seen as one who guards the doorway, and one who possesses the inner secrets hidden from the profane. The vervain blossom is a sign of the lasting covenant with the Witch as the steward of Nature.

In the Moon's Light

Ancient Roman writers, such as Horace, wrote of Witches drawing the moon down from the heavens. Indeed the literature of Witchcraft depicts an intimate relationship between the moon and Witches. It is clear that a belief has long existed concerning Witches obtaining power from the light of the moon.

In Charles Leland's *Aradia: Gospel of the Witches* (1899) we find a reference to Witches gathering beneath the moon:

> Whenever ye have need of anything, once in the month and when the moon is full, ye shall assemble

in some secret place, or in a forest all together join to adore the potent spirit of your queen, my mother, great Diana. She who fain would learn all sorcery yet has not won its deepest secrets, them my mother will teach her, in truth all things as yet unknown. And ye shall be freed from slavery, and so ye shall be free in everything; and as a sign that ye are truly free, ye shall be naked in your rites, both men and women also . . . [2]

The full moon has called to something in the human spirit as long ago as the Neolithic period, if not much earlier. Images of the moon displaying a full circle, flanked by left and right facing crescents, appear in primitive art as early as 4500–4300 B.C.E. A coiled serpent flanked by these crescent shapes also appears during the same period, and, as noted earlier, one of the goddesses associated with Witchcraft (Proserpina) is intimately linked with the serpent.

Several writers of the classical era wrote that the moon's light made plants and animals fertile. The morning dew itself was believed to be a magical water left by moonlight, and a popular folk magic belief held that a woman could be made fertile by sleeping nude in a meadow beneath the full moon and awakening covered in the morning dew. It is interesting to note that in the Aegean/Mediterranean region the Moon Goddess was also known as the All-Dewy-One.

The Goddess of the Moon was originally worshipped in groves where a lake or a spring could be found. She was also worshipped in a grotto where water issued forth from between the rocks. Her priestesses bore the responsibility of caring for the sacred water within the grove or grotto. Traditionally a sacred fire was tended, which represented the moon's own light, and this fire could not be allowed to go out, due to an ancient belief that the Moon Goddess was the light of the fire itself.

As noted in chapter two, in ancient times it was held that fire lies latent in wood. The security of the Divine fire required an ample supply of sacred wood, which was dried and kept readily available in the grove or grotto of the Moon Goddess. Later in history, lamps replaced the need for wood, but the link was never truly severed because the lamp fuel was often the oil extracted from olive trees.

There is an interesting legend in which the Goddess Diana is smuggled out of Greece inside a bundle of olive branches and delivered to Lake Nemi in Italy. Thus Diana was the latent flame within the wood, awaiting rebirth in her new grove. The bundle of branches in which she arrived was the first supply of her sacred grove torches.

The Moon Goddess, as a mythological being, belongs to the torch-bearing class of deities who themselves were always connected in some manner with the Underworld. The Underworld connection linked the Moon Goddess to the Fates, and thus the power of divination was bestowed upon her worshippers by the light of the moon itself and by the torches that represented the moon's light. To this day many Witches perform divination by candlelight.

The essential reasons why Witches originally gathered beneath the full moon are related to the moon's light. Just as flame within the wood could be awakened (the goddess within), so too could the "inner light" or spirit of the worshippers be awakened by the full moon. Although the ancient belief held that the light of the full moon could impart fertility, the fertility they desired was not only of the body, it was also of the mind and spirit. This is reflected in one of the traditional closing ritual prayers of a full moon ceremony:

> . . . When our bodies lie resting nightly, speak to our
> inner spirits, teach us all Your Holy Mysteries. I be-
> lieve Your ancient promise that we who seek Your
> Holy Presence will receive of Your wisdom. Behold,

O'Ancient Goddess, we have gathered beneath the Full Moon at this appointed time. Now the Full Moon shines upon us. Hear us. Recall Your ancient promise. . . .

The Witch As Priest(ess)

As mentioned earlier in this book, the Witch is one of the Hidden Children of the Goddess, a secret one of the chosen few. We know that throughout the world primitive communities had their shaman, medicine man, or witch doctor figure. These were individuals who possessed certain qualities that made their fellow tribe members regard them as being in contact with the spirit world. Something about these individuals also made them appear to have certain powers that the average tribe member did not possess or demonstrate. In many regions of Europe this figure was the Witch.

It requires no leap of logic to conclude that the Witch, a person in communication with the spirit realm, would direct and preside over the community rituals. Such a role evolved over time, rendering the Witch as a priest or priestess figure. The ancient tale of the Witch Medea portraying her as a priestess of Hecate is one example that supports the existence of this theme as one of great antiquity.

The Witch is a priest(ess) of the Old Ways, a term referring to practices and beliefs that are in harmonious accord with Nature and its hidden secrets. The Witch is also a priest(ess) of the moon, for the moon is a symbol of enlightenment in the darkness. Darkness conceals and obscures that which it envelops, but the light of the moon reveals the form of things hidden in the darkness. The Witch, as an agent of the moon, is one who sees in the night and can discern the hidden and obscure. It was for this reason that people sought out the Witch as a fortune-teller.

In addition to the celestial connection, the Witch is also a priest(ess) of the old gods of field and forest. The horned god of fertility and the spirit of the woods known as the Green Man is still revered by the priests and priestesses of the Old Ways. In modern times it has been suggested that Witches are the clergy for the Pagan community. If this is true today, then it simply reflects the older role of the Witch in his or her community.

Unlike many other religions the priest(ess) does not mediate between the deity and worshipper. In Witchcraft as a religion, the role of priest(ess) is more a personal relationship or dedication to deity than it is an office per se. Because of this perspective, most Witches will in time become priests or priestesses.

In many Traditions the priest(ess) serves as an advisor and counselor in her/his community. The priest(ess) will also typically serve as a facilitator during the ritual occasions of the year and the monthly full moons. In most cases the priest(ess) will be devoted to a specific god and goddess, although some individuals prefer to use the terms "the Goddess" and "the God" instead of personifying the concept by using any specific name related to any particular culture.

Another role that the priest(ess) serves is to ensure the turning of the Wheel of the Year. As previously noted, the Wheel of the Year is a phrase that refers to the seasonal rites in Witchcraft. When we examine ancient beliefs we find that our ancestors thought it necessary to assist such things as the return of the sun's warmth when Winter came, the return of Spring, and the fertility of plants and animals. This worldview resulted in the tradition of Witches "Turning the Wheel" through the unbroken performance of the eight seasonal rites.

According to an old legend, a Witch grew in power by performing the rituals of Witchcraft. Unbroken devotion to the full moon rituals and the seasonal rites bestowed (and maintained) the Witch's powers. On the following page is a list of the legendary powers of the Witch.

- To bring success in matters of love.

- To bless and consecrate.

- To speak with spirits.

- To know the hidden things.

- To call forth spirits.

- To know the voice of the wind.

- To possess the knowledge of transformation.

- To possess the knowledge of divination.

- To know and understand secret signs.

- To cure disease.

- To bring forth the glamour of beauty.

- To have influence over wild beasts.

- To know the secrets of the hands.

The Voice of the Wind

There is an old belief in Witchcraft that people can be "spirit taught" by hearing the "voice of the wind." This term denotes several things related to the tenets of Witchcraft. It is often used when speaking of intuitive/psychic abilities, and when referring to a person who feels directed, inspired, or to one who "channels" a spirit/entity that speaks directly through the individual. Hearing the voice of the wind is sometimes used to indicate that a person hears the voices of spirits or fairies.

The term "voice of the wind" can also mean that a person has accessed the Akashic Records and is tapping into ancient memories. The Akashic Records is a term referring to a magnetic/etheric plane in which the energy patterns of all that has transpired on our planet are imprinted within the magnetic mantle surrounding the Earth. This is not unlike data being stored on magnetic computer disks.

Occultists believe that the energy imprints contained within the Akashic Records can be accessed through magical and psychic methods. In occultism the Akashic Records are often envisioned as an immense library containing the collective records of the ages that have passed on the Earth. Spontaneous knowledge can be transmitted to anyone who successfully taps into the magnetically recorded and stored patterns.

The World Between the Worlds

In Witchcraft there is an old belief that a realm exists in-between the world of the living and the world that lies beyond. Casting a magical ritual circle according to prescribed methods can create an access point to this anteroom or corridor. In some Traditions the circle itself, once properly cast, is said to then lie between the worlds.

Some Witches believe that this place is the elemental realm where the spirits of Earth, Air, Fire, and Water dwell (see chapter eight). Others believe it is a realm that lies between the elemental and astral realms. The former concept may originate from a belief in the "fairy doorway" of European folklore. Fairies have often been identified with the elemental spirits and it can be difficult to distinguish between the two in popular lore.

The value of the existence of a "world between the worlds" lies in the belief that magic is most effective when created directly within this realm. The atmosphere of this realm is not contaminated with the disbelief and skepticism found in the world of humankind. Therefore the power of magic is not encumbered by any doubt in its existence.

Being between the worlds places one in the unique position of not being entirely subject to the laws and ways of any one of the seven planes of existence: ultimate, divine, spiritual, mental, astral, elemental, and physical. This allows one a certain freedom of experimentation that might otherwise have lasting effects in any other realm. The world between the worlds is, in effect, your own microcosmic universe over which you preside. For further information on the planes, see chapter nine.

The Witch as Spiritual Warrior

It can be said that the Witch dwells between the worlds, for he or she is one who lives in both the mundane world and the so-called supernatural world. The Witch is, among many things, a spiritual warrior on a sacred quest. He or she carries the weapons of a mystical knight. In a metaphorical sense the Witch's chalice is the helmet, the pentacle the shield, the wand a lance, and the athame a sword. The quest of the Witch is to discover his or her place in the three great mysteries, which are discussed in detail in chapter nine.

At the core of the spiritual warrior is the personal code and the steadfast determination to hold to what one believes is right. The mentality of the Witch as a spiritual warrior is best summed up in the key words of the Master: *to know, to will, to dare, and to be silent.*

To know is the basis of knowledge, and one's opinion and perspective should be an informed one. Therefore the Witch must do more than satisfy mere curiosity concerning any one subject of interest. He or she must study not only the subject itself but also those things that relate to the concepts that enrich the understanding of the subject.

To will is to endure without yielding to defeat or discouragement. The spiritual warrior must walk his or her path despite its obstacles and hardships. To dare, the Witch must be willing to accept the risks of disfavor and mistreatment that arise from one's adversaries. The spiritual warrior must be true to the path he or she walks, whether the road is smooth and safe or risky and covered with pitfalls. To be silent, the spiritual warrior must simply speak his or her truths without argument or hidden agenda.

The Three Bodies

The belief exists that we are comprised of essentially three inner selves: the lower, middle, and higher. The lower self is concerned with the mundane aspects of physical existence. In other words, the lower self oversees all that the five physical senses and emotional needs bring to our lives. The middle self is where our intellect and individuality expresses itself. It may give in to the demands and cravings of the lower self, compromise/negotiate with it, or strive to control and direct it as much as possible. The higher self is the presence of the soul and its connection to divinity or the "divine spark" within us.

All three aspects of the self have their unique needs and requirements. When these are not met, the result is an imbalance. Imbalance creates disharmony and affects one's spiritual state of being. Whenever this occurs, then one or more of the bodies will react. Depending upon which body is in imbalance, the mood or disposition of the individual will fluctuate. The purpose here is to draw the attention of the individual so that he or she will take corrective measures to restore balance. For the Witch, the spiritual walk is all about balance.

The Witch understands that everything on both the material and spiritual level is interconnected. When one thing changes, it creates a ripple that changes everything else. Therefore the Witch feels that it is vital to live and act in accord with Nature. Here the Witch participates with life rather than being a victim of life.

At the core of the Witch's code is the acceptance of responsibility for his or her own actions. The Witch does not blame his or her life situation on others. The Witch understands that every personal action or lack of action causes or allows something to manifest. Therefore, the individual ultimately shapes their life.

Let us turn now to the next chapter and explore how the Witch lives and works in the mundane world of everyday life on planet Earth.

SIX

The Witch in Daylight

M any people would be greatly surprised to discover that their mail carrier, neighborhood police officer, primary physician, schoolteacher, or attorney is a practicing Witch. However it is true that Witches can be found (and are found) in these and other professions. Some Witches also serve in the military, defending the freedom and security of their nation.

One of the freedoms that Witches strongly believe in is the freedom of religion. To the Witch, freedom of religion includes all religions, whether they are Christian, Islamic, Buddhist, Judaism, Paganism, or whatever. Unfortunately there are still many places in the world where Witches cannot be public regarding their religion because of the ignorance that often surrounds the subject of Witchcraft.

Public education is important and many Witches work very hard to dispel the erroneous views that are fostered (both intentionally and unintentionally) by the media, television shows, movies, and by certain religious groups who view themselves as the only correct worshippers of the one true "God." Bias and personal agenda are often at the core of the ongoing persecution of Witches.

Most non-Witches grew up with the fairy-tale image of the wicked Witch, and later encountered the notion of the "evil Witch" as depicted by the Christian Church during the era of the Inquisition. Here the Church sanctioned the torture of anyone suspected of practicing Witchcraft, as well as the killing of anyone who was convicted of the charge. Ironically the vast majority of these individuals were not Witches by any definition of the word. They were simply the victims of religious intolerance.

With the release of the movie *The Wizard of Oz*, the average person was first presented with the concept of a "good witch" and a "bad witch." In reality there aren't any bad witches or good witches, there are only good people and bad people. This is because religion alone cannot make you a good person or a bad person. Regretfully the actions of a few can reflect badly upon the whole, and this is not unique to Witches and Witchcraft. In the news we encounter evangelical ministers who are caught with prostitutes, Catholic priests molesting children, and so forth. These acts are not sanctioned by the religion that these individuals profess to practice, but are instead the actions of isolated individuals.

Witches, like the vast majority of religious people, are essentially good folks who hold jobs, raise families, abide by the laws of the land, pay taxes, vote, and seek to live in peace with their neighbors. Witches do not, by personal desire or religious creed, sacrifice animals or humans. Witches respect life and the rights of others to live their own lives unmolested. Witches do not worship a deity devoted to evil, nor do they wish to harm the innocent.

Self-Responsibility

One of the core tenets of Witchcraft is the acceptance of responsibility for one's behavior, words, and actions. In the theology of Witchcraft there is no entity who tries to tempt, mislead, trick, or deceive practitioners in any way. Witches do not typically believe that deity creates hardships through which to test the "faith" of individuals. It is also not a tenet of Witchcraft that deity punishes its worshippers, nor allows them to suffer for eternity. Instead the gods and goddesses of Witchcraft ensure (in many interesting ways) that their followers confront themselves and make those changes that are necessary for spiritual growth.

Witches essentially believe that one's actions create a "cause and effect" situation that will ultimately influence future events surrounding the person that initiated the act. Positive actions draw positive returns, and negative actions draw negative returns, for in Witchcraft there is a maxim that states "Like attracts like."

Witches do not strive to live a certain way in order to obtain rewards, nor do they avoid certain behaviors so as to avert penalties. Witches live life in accord with a personal code of honor and a practical sense of what is right and wrong behavior within a community. Witches believe in peaceful coexistence whenever and wherever possible. However, most Witches are not typically pacifists or a "turn the other cheek" kind of people by any stretch of the imagination. Witches hold other people accountable for their behavior, just as Witches do regarding themselves.

In some modern Witchcraft Traditions there is an adage known as the "Three-fold Law of Return." This principle is based upon an occult tenet of cause and effect. Essentially any act that a person performs effects him or her on three levels: the mind, body, and spirit. Let's consider this principle further by example.

Picture a person who has observed an old man walking down the street. The old person unknowingly drops a large wad of money from his pocket and continues to walk along. The other person now has two basic choices: retrieve the cash and give it back to the old man, or pick up the cash and quietly slip away with it. The conscious act (mind) creates an emotional response within the person. The emotional response triggers a reaction from the endocrine system, which affects the body (fear, delight, anxiety, etc.). Now that the mind and body have been influenced, the arousal of energy and the reaction of mind and body likewise affect the indwelling spirit or soul of the person. Therefore the individual has been affected on three levels by one action.

Some Witches view the Three-Fold Law in a different way. These individuals believe that an action is an energy that draws back to itself three times the intensity of the initial force. In other words, whatever one does (good or bad) comes back three times as strong in effect. There is, however, no corresponding principle in the law of physics to match this concept. Basically speaking, if you throw a rock up in the air, it comes back down with the same force as it went up with. This is because the pull of gravity is equal on both the ascent and the descent—therefore it does not come back down with three times the force.

Code of Ethics

In many modern Traditions of Witchcraft there is a precept called "The Rede" which essentially states: "As it harm none, do as thou wilt." Many Witches interpret the meaning of this tenet differently. Some believe that it means a person can do whatever he or she desires as long as no one else is harmed as a result. Others believe it is a guideline for exercising caution in one's mundane and magical dealings, and is not an iron-clad rule. There are probably as many interpretations of the Rede as there are Witchcraft Traditions.

The original public version of the Rede read: "Eight words the Witches' Rede fulfill: An ye harm none, do what ye will."

Several years later an addition appeared, which read: "Lest in thy self-defense it be, ever mind the rule of Three. Follow this with mind and heart, and merry ye meet, and merry ye part."

In the older forms of Witchcraft, dating from antiquity, no such concept of the Rede existed. Ancient Witches were like the untamed creatures living free in Nature. They preferred to avoid confrontation, but if challenged anything was possible. If cornered and left no avenue of escape, then an unrestrained fight was inevitable. The Witch was a valuable ally to friends and a formidable foe to enemies. It would be difficult to examine any ancient culture and not find essentially the same mentality related to any ancient people.

Witchcraft, like any religion, has evolved over the centuries and has adapted to the cultural environment in which it found itself. Witches too have changed over the years, and few practice a pure and entirely unaltered form of the ancient ways. However the true and free spirit of the Witch remains unshackled.

The modern Witch holds to a basic worldview in which he or she operates. His or her personal codes are not based upon "morality" or the lack thereof, for these are things dictated by the social order, which requires individuals to conform to pre-established external creeds. Instead the Witch possesses his or her own heartfelt truths, and does not pretend to follow the truths that others would impose. I have designed the codes presented here to capture and reflect the general spirit of the Witch:

- I do not force my will upon others because it is the actions of others that call forth the response of my will.

- I do not desire power over others because I know I possess personal power and am secure in that realization.

- I return the intent of what is given or sent to me, whether good or bad, because I seek freedom from attachment.

- I do not harm the innocent, because my enemies choose provocation.

- I do not steal because what belongs to me is what I have earned.

- I do not take a life other than to preserve life, because I am part of Nature.

- I do not secretly thrust my pitchfork into another's harvest because mine is work enough. There is no honor in a gain that is undeserved.

- I do not modify my beliefs and convictions for the convenience of others or myself because I rely upon being who I am.

- I do not lie because I rely upon truth (in myself and in others). Where there is no truth, each word is wasted energy, and I never misuse energy.

- I do not betray those I love because I would not cut off my hand, or foot, or nose, or any part of me that I cherish.

- I am not untrustworthy because my word, once given, is my oath to which I am bound, and I never betray myself.

- I do not live in fear nor self-impose my limitations because I do not accept the domination of others over my life.

- I do not play the role of victim because I am too busy participating in my life and shaping my own future.

- I do not worship in the ways others would have me do because Nature is my first and truest love.

- I venerate the old gods because they do not demand it, but my own heart does.

Stewardship of Nature

Witches are people who seek balance in both worlds, the spiritual and the mundane. Because Witches perceive of themselves as the stewards of Nature (a spiritual calling), they typically become involved in environmental concerns. This can range from actions as humble as simply recycling waste accumulated in the home, to something as large as serving on the front lines with organizations that confront those corporations that view the earth as their personal trash receptacle.

I know many Witches who take garbage bags to parks, beaches, and roadsides where they pick up other people's trash. Some Witches become active in organizations that work to protect natural resources such as forests, lakes, rivers, and wildlife areas. Sadly we all live in a world that is financially and politically controlled by those who look at a beautiful meadow and see only "undeveloped land" that would make a nice location for a shopping center. They look at majestic forests and see paper products, furniture, and building material. To such individuals the rivers are essentially convenient, low cost, running toilet water, and the oceans are little more than sewage and waste areas.

The Witch sees in Nature that which is necessary for life to continue. The Witch understands that what becomes of the earth happens to us all. There is no separation, and we are all part of the design. Unfortunately a relatively small handful of people, driven by financial gain, are able to destroy the rain forests that produce most of the world's oxygen, contaminate the soil that produces the food we eat, and pollute the air that we breath with toxins.

The Witch does not consider immediate financial gain as justification for destroying a world and robbing future generations of the beauty of life on this planet. Perhaps life on earth may continue once the forests are gone and bodies of water are little more than chemical pools and streams. In such a world, cities may be encased in environmental bubbles containing a manufactured atmosphere. Theme parks of this era will attract people by bringing them into contact with trees, birds, and a few assorted animals as a reminder of what once was, in our distant past.

Since 1989, scientists have been engaged in a significant study of frogs as an indicator of environmental conditions. This study arose from the discovery that frog populations were mysteriously disappearing in many regions of the world, and large numbers of frog populations were showing up with physical deformities.

Scientists have advanced a number of theories in an attempt to explain the deformities. Prime suspects include chemical contamination as well as increased ultraviolet radiation due to ozone depletion. While some people may not be concerned about what happens to frogs, there are many indications that humans are being affected as well.

A 1996 study by University of Minnesota researchers (EHP 104[4]: 394–399) showed an increased incidence of abnormality and chromosomal aberration among children born to workers that apply pesticides in Minnesota. In western Minnesota (a major wheat, sugar beet, and potato-growing region) the rate of incidents increased sharply for children conceived in the spring, which is the time of heaviest pesticide application.

Many of the sites in which deformed frogs have been discovered are close to farm fields that are intensively sprayed with pesticides and herbicides at certain times of the year. Frogs spend a major portion of their lives in water, and are therefore particularly vulnerable to the ill effects stemming from the chemical contamination of water. Scientists have noted that 60 percent of the frog population in agricultural areas show deformities.

The fungicide Maneb and propylthiourea, a pesticide, were shown to cause limb malformations in frogs under laboratory conditions. There are several other chemical agents known to cause gross anatomical deformities in wildlife, such as high levels of selenium leaching into surface water, which causes defects in the eggs of shorebirds and fish. Dioxin and dioxin-related chemicals (now found in the Great Lakes of the United States) are suspected of causing deformed bills among fish-eating birds.

The thyroid gland plays a significant part in controlling frog metamorphosis. It has been demonstrated that adding thyroid hormone to pond water and sediment greatly reduces the number of malformations in frogs. This strongly suggests that man-made chemicals may be disrupting the endocrine system in frogs and interfering with the process of normal development.

It is interesting to note that the frog and the Witch have been associated with one another for many centuries. In viewing the Witch as a steward of nature the relationship here seems quite striking. There is much work for the Witch to do related to preservation. The future will be the harvest, rich or poor, of what we plant or fail to plant (both literally and figuratively) today.

Even on a small scale, the Witch can contribute to preserving many things. Plant some trees, create a garden, build a pond, feed wildlife, and contribute anyway you can to organizations that work to preserve Nature and the diversity of life within it. If you are a Witch, or choose to become one, then the chances are that you have reincarnated at this time in the world to help save our planet.

Check with local organizations and agencies to see if you can help replant areas burned away in wildfires. Search the Internet for organizations that you would want to become involved with. If you cannot become involved yourself, then try to motivate others. Make your views on environmental protection and preservation known to your governmental representatives.

Self-Discipline

Part of being a Witch is the development of the powers of your mind. This requires personal effort and self-discipline. Two very common and fundamental phrases that appear in Witchcraft are "as my will, so mote it be" and "by my word, so mote it be." These sayings are used to affirm the outcome of words just previously spoken, such as "And may my wish come true, and as I will so mote it be!" The use of "word" and "will" both reflect the core concept of discipline in the practice of Witchcraft.

If you have ever known someone with such determination that they never give up until they achieve their goal, then you know how impressive that can be. This type of person obtains a reputation, and when he or she lets it be known that a quest to fulfill a desire is in motion, everyone accepts that it will happen. People with experiential knowledge of such a person will often make a conscious decision not to struggle against him or her, or to assist him or her if only to save time and energy.

In a magical sense, the Witch must develop his or her will so it becomes a powerful personal tool. Once the will is strengthened to the point where it does not concede defeat, then it can aid the Witch in his or her magical and ritual work. When the people and the spirits you work with believe in the strength of your will because of its reality, then they will react to the statement that your will is behind the outcome you desire. Likewise the word of the Witch must also be unshakable, and once given it must be followed through with. If your word means nothing to you, it will mean nothing to the people and spirits around you.

Even if you would not define yourself as strong-willed, you can develop the trait over time. To begin, start with small and easily attained goals. This can be something as simple as building a basic plastic model from a hobby kit, or completing a "paint-by-numbers" art piece. Designate specific days and times to work, and then make sure you adhere to the schedule. Once you have successfully accomplished small goals, then move on to more complex and difficult tasks. If you're like most people, you will become frustrated and you will want to stop short of your goal at some point. Pushing past this will be the turning point, so try not to let yourself down by surrendering. You can never fail until you actually stop trying.

Keeping your word is very important, for it must have the same power as your will. Bear in mind that there is a difference between saying you will do such and such, and giving your word that you will do such and such. Giving one's word means you will do what you stated despite anything that arises to thwart your intent. Therefore you will want to make it clear to people whether you are saying "I intend to be there" as opposed to "I give you my word I will be there." One of the easiest ways to keep your word is to never give it unless you know with certainty that you can fulfill it.

Another part of crafting self-discipline is to embrace something like yoga, archery, martial arts, or the mastery of a musical instrument, etc. The key here is to make this a spiritual exercise that is more about developing "you" than it is about becoming good at what you choose to do.

At some point you may wish to add a deeper spiritual element related to self-discipline. One example would be to take lessons and learn to play the flute as an offering to the God and Goddess. Once you become good at the flute, then you only play it for ritual, magical, or devotional purposes. In this way your music is always an intimate and special offering.

An Abundant Life

Unlike some of the other world religions, Witchcraft does not advocate a life of poverty or detachment from material goods. Most Witches believe in fruitfulness and in living a happy, prosperous, and purposeful life. However, Witchcraft is not a path devoted to riches, power, and fame. It is instead a religion devoted to manifesting the full potential of all of its practitioners on both the material and spiritual levels.

As a Witch it is very important that you maintain a positive outlook on both the present and the future. Try to avoid using the word "can't" to describe your goals or abilities. For example, if you are not confident in your artistic abilities do not say "I can't draw" or "I can't paint." Instead use the phrase "I don't currently possess the experience to draw well." Apply this general philosophy to your goals as well.

The old saying, "like attracts like" best illustrates an important magical principle. What this means is that things of a similar nature attract one another. From a metaphysical perspective this formula envisions that any specific energy is drawn to other forms of energy with which it is harmonious.

Therefore, in a simplistic sense, negative energy draws more negative energy and positive energy attracts more positive energy. Magically speaking, thoughts are things in and of themselves, and they have an energy vibration. Whatever you dwell on—good or bad—you will attract more of the same to yourself.

You can help create abundance, success, and prosperity in your life by decorating your home with symbols that reflect your goals and desires. Choose color themes of green to represent growth. Light browns and beige create stability and foundation. Light to medium blue is good for peace and harmony. Avoid yellow and red in the home as these are stimulating and tend to encumber the recuperative qualities of hearth and home.

Statues of agricultural deities associated with grain are good choices for home decor and altar focus. Fertility deities should also be placed in the home. Avoid placing them in the west area of your home as the west is associated with departure. The east or the north are good choices for gain.

To increase your focus on success and prosperity, set up a personal shrine in the east area of your home. This can be a shelf, desk top, or any flat surface. Your prosperity shrine should contain a green candle for you to light every day as an affirmation of your participation in your own success and gain. Place three coins on the shrine to symbolize material gain. Set a small holder for containing dried grain. This will symbolize grow and renewal. Replenish the grain once a month when the moon is full.

Any good-luck charms you find or receive should be placed on your shrine. You can even place an encouraging "fortune cookie" message on your shrine. In essence the shrine becomes a focal point for affirming your goals and staying focused on feelings of good and productive energy. You should spent a few moments everyday mentally connecting with your shrine and its symbology.

It is important to understand that your thoughts have a ripple effect. They not only influence your general disposition but in turn affect the energy of your aura, which is the energy field surrounding your physical body. The aura emanates an energy field that is the accumulation (in vibratory quality) of your mental, physical, and spiritual state of being. Therefore you will find that people and situations that possess the same type of energy vibration will be drawn to you. This is something that you can change or encourage as needed or desired. See chapter nine for further information on this principle.

The Arts of Witchcraft

To round out your preliminary training as a Witch, it is advisable to study one or more of the traditional arts of Witchcraft. These arts include herbalism, tarot, palmistry, crystal gazing, magic, and the preparation of oils and incenses. In addition to one of these arts, you may also, at some point, want to include one of the related arts such as ritual tool making, sewing robes, candle making, creating poppets, and making amulets or other occult jewelry.

The traditional arts of Witchcraft fall into the categories of divination, healing, and spirit work. These timeless practices have brought the Witch into the public arena as a counselor, advisor, and cleric. In the oral tradition of Witchcraft, Witches were the local wisewomen and wise men who were sought out to cure illness, make magical potions and charms, foretell the future, and appease spirits from the Otherworld.

Many modern Witches serve their communities by performing divination with Tarot cards, runes, or palmistry. The average occult store or "Witch Shop" will typically have a "reader" available to the public. Most Witches offer more than just the reading and interpretation of the cards, runes, or lines of the hand. The Witch will often guide the person having the reading into an understanding of his or her role in the state of affairs, and suggest ways to improve things in a healthy manner.

Now that we have looked at some of the things Witches use to communicate with the Otherworld, let us turn to the next chapter and explore the classic tools of Witchcraft.

SEVEN

The Tools of Witchcraft

In the religion of Witchcraft certain tools are used for ritual and magical purposes. These traditional tools include a blade called an athame, a platter known as a pentacle, a wand, and a chalice. In some traditions a small scourge and a sword are also used.

The use of such tools appears to be of quite great antiquity and is found in the ancient cult of Mithras. As author Robert Turcan noted in his book *The Cults of the Roman Empire*, the symbolic tools of Mithraism were the wand of command, the libation cup, the platter, the crescent-shaped knife, the sword, and the Sun's whip. The main rituals of Mithraism were centered around a sacramental meal, which is also true of the primary Witchcraft rituals.[1]

Witchcraft rituals are performed in large circles marked upon the ground. The traditional circles measured eighteen feet in diameter, while many modern circles measure about nine feet across. In modern Witchcraft the ritual circle is often referred to as "sacred space." The circle is always cast in a clockwise motion, using either the athame or the wand to trace along the circle's edge. This motion is called *deosil*, which means moving with the sun. When a ritual is completed, the circle is then traced again, but this time in a counterclockwise motion. This movement is called *widdershins*, which means against the sun.

The altar is placed at or near the center of the circle. The altar itself is a focal point, a place of reverence through which one can approach his or her individual understanding of deity. In some Traditions the altar is oriented to the viewer so that he or she faces east, and in other Traditions the orientation is to the north.

The traditional Witches' altar is round in shape, symbolizing the cycles of Nature. In modern Witchcraft many Witches use altars that are rectangular, symbolizing the Underworld and Overworld supported by the columns of light and darkness. Some Traditions use a cubical altar, representing the four elements of creation united in harmony. In ancient times large flat rocks were used as altars, as were tree stumps. Some rocks were large enough for a woman to recline upon, serving symbolically as the living altar of the Goddess Herself.

Setting up the altar is an important part of any ritual. It should be performed with focus and concentration upon the inner meanings as each item is placed on the altar. In effect, the Witch is creating his or her own microcosm of the Universe as the tools are laid out upon the altar. In a magical sense the altar serves as the "battery" for the ritual or magical work at hand. A well-established altar serves as a catalyst to the magical states of consciousness necessary for effective rituals.

The Witches' altar is sprinkled with purified water containing three pinches of salt. Incense smoke (such as sandalwood or frangipani) is passed over the altar to further cleanse it. Many modern Witches use sage smudge sticks. The Witch speaks aloud the intent to erect an altar, purify it, and verbally dedicates it to a specific ritual intent and deity name.

Traditionally a black cloth is spread over the altar to symbolize the darkness of procreation, from which all things manifest. A candle representing the Goddess is set at the upper-left section of the altar, and another candle to represent the God is placed at the upper-right section. Statues of the Goddess and God are placed next to these candles accordingly. This portrays the presence of the God and Goddess overseeing the process of creation reflected in the altar setup as it proceeds. See appendix three for more information.

The ritual tools are arranged on the center of the altar according to their elemental nature. Here they form a circle with the pentacle in the top section, the wand on the right, athame on the bottom, and the chalice to the left. In some Witchcraft Traditions the elemental assignment of the tools differs from those given here. Therefore, the pattern of laying out the tools would be different.

In addition to the classic tools, a basic altar typically incorporates an incense burner, candle extinguisher, container of purified water, a silver ritual bell, and decorations associated with the season of the year. These are usually arranged according to personal taste and eye for design.

Spring altars are often adorned with flowers. Summer altars are set with fruit and a variety of flowers. Fall altars are frequently decorated with pine cones, acorns, or symbols of the harvest. Winter altars are customarily ornamented with wreaths of holly and other traditional Yule symbolism.

Concerning the Tools

The earliest public depiction of the four tools (appearing together in a magical/ritual context) is found in the fifteenth-century Italian Tarot deck now known as the Cary-Yale Visconti deck. With the exception of the chalice, these ritual tools also appear in a medieval book of ceremonial magic known as the *Key of Solomon*. It is interesting to note that in the home of an accused Witch named Laura Malipero (Venice, 1640), a copy of the *Key of Solomon* was discovered, along with a personal spell book into which she was copying various sections from the *Key*.

The four tools used in Witchcraft constitute a set of spiritual implements for religious and ritual purposes. In occultism certain virtues are assigned to the ritual tools. The pentacle is the shield of valor. The wand is the lance of intuition. The blade is the sword of reason, and the chalice is the well of compassion. In such a view the four tools become the weapons of the spiritual knight or warrior (see chapter five).

The four tools of Witchcraft: the Athame, the Wand, the Cup, and the Pentacle.

The wand and the chalice are the oldest tools of Witchcraft. The wand is derived from the sacred branch taken from the divine tree within the sacred grove. The chalice is derived from the use of gourds or shells to collect rainwater and dew, fluids sacred to the moon.

The ritual blade was a later addition to the tools of Witchcraft. It was developed around the same time as the pentacle. Both tools are associated with the theme of the Slain God and the use of blade and platter. The pentacle platter is made of stone or clay and represents Earth. The wand represents Air in its association with the tree branch. The blade represents Fire as it is forged in fire. The chalice represents Water as it symbolizes the womb.

The Pentacle

The pentacle is traditionally made of stone or clay, and is a tool of elemental Earth. Some Witches prefer a metal pentacle because of its durability, and since it is made of elements taken from the earth it does not lose its basic connection. Some Witches use pentacles made of wood, which is difficult to reconcile with traditional occult principles.

Typically most pentacles are about six to twelve inches in diameter, although pentacles can be found in any size due to personal tastes. The basic pentacle bears on its surface a large five-pointed star known as a pentagram. On the pentacle the star symbolizes the active principle of the four elements kept in balance by the presence of spirit (the fifth element). Here it is bound to the pentacle, which symbolizes the material realm. Through this symbolism the Witch wields the creative powers of the four elements in his or her hands.

The pentacle can be prepared for use by sprinkling it with some salted water, and then passing it three times through some incense smoke. This cleanses its energy of anything that might have contaminated the pentacle prior to your ownership. For additional purification you can set the pentacle out in the sunlight at noon for one hour.

Once the pentacle has been purified it can then be dedicated to the service of the Goddess and the God. This is a simple procedure that requires anointing the pentacle with a dab of mineral oil on the outer rim, which is then traced along the edge with one's finger (completing one full circling). Then beginning at the top point of the star, and moving downward, the star is traced with a dab of oil in a clockwise fashion.

While tracing the star, the Witch recites:

> Witches' star of ancient magic power,
> Come, awaken now in this shadowed hour.
> Manifest each desire, call, and wish,
> In the name of the God and of the Goddess.

The Wand

As noted earlier, the wand is made of wood and is a tool of elemental Air (in some Traditions it is assigned to Fire). Traditionally the wand is made from one of the sacred trees of Witchcraft. The most popular wood for a wand is oak, but many Witches favor a willow, beech, rowan, or ash.

The time-honored custom concerning the wand requires its length to be personalized according to the individual Witch. The wand is measured by a portion of the left arm, and should extend in length from the inside of the elbow to the tip of the middle finger. This aligns the wand with its owner and helps establish an intimate connection.

The wand can be prepared for use by sprinkling it with some salted water, and then passing it three times through some incense smoke. For additional purification the wand can be set out in the sunlight at noon for one hour. After removing it from the sunlight, the wand is lightly rubbed down with a small amount of linseed oil.

Once the wand has been purified, it can then be marked with any symbols one might want to place upon its shaft. Before proceeding with this stage the linseed oil must first have time to penetrate and become absorbed. The wand may need to be wiped with a dry cotton cloth before painting or carving symbols in the wood.

The final step is to dedicate the wand to the service of the Goddess and the God. This is a simple procedure that requires anointing the wand on the tip and shaft with three drops each of camphor oil, heliotrope oil, and patchouli oil. The oil is worked into the wood with one's hands so that the entire tool from top to bottom is covered with a fine surface coating.

When the wand is ready, it is held up to the full moon. While the wand is moved in a circular motion as though it were slowly circling around the moon, the Witch recites:

> Witches' wand of ancient magic power,
> Come, awaken now in this shadowed hour.
> Summon each desire, call, and wish,
> In the name of the God and of the Goddess.

The Athame

The athame is made of a steel blade and bears a black handle. The handle can be made of wood or animal horn. The athame is a tool of elemental Fire (in some Traditions it is assigned to Air). Traditionally the blade can never have drawn blood before the Witch possesses it, and must never be allowed to draw blood afterward.

The athame can be prepared for use by sprinkling it with some salted water, and then passing it three times through some incense smoke. For additional purification the athame can be set out in the sunlight at noon for one hour. After removing it from the sunlight, the athame is lightly rubbed with a small dab of mineral oil, which is then wiped clean with a cotton cloth.

Once the athame has been purified, it can then be charged with fire by placing the blade directly in a candle flame for a few minutes. Once the blade is quite hot, the Witch recites the following, and then quickly dips the blade into a bowl of cold water:

> Witches' blade of ancient magic power,
> Come, awaken now in this shadowed hour.
> Banish all that I request and wish,
> In the name of the God and of the Goddess.

Next the blade is dried off with a cotton cloth, and then charged with a magnet, which is repeatedly stroked along the blade from base to tip (always moving in one direction only, never back and forth). While performing this charge the Witch recites:

> Witches' blade of ancient magic power,
> Come, awaken now in this shadowed hour.
> Draw each desire, call, and wish,
> In the name of the God and of the Goddess.

The final step is to dedicate the athame to the service of the Goddess and the God. On the night of the full moon, a small hole is dug about six inches deep, and then filled up again with the loose soft soil (gently patted down). The Witch kneels in front of the spot, grasps the handle of the athame and raises it up to the moon (blade pointed down). Next the Witch speaks the following, and firmly yet slowly lowers the blade of the athame into the soil, pushing it down to the hilt:

> From above where light is full and round,
> By blade and will I draw Thee down.
> The sky and earth are bound to blade,
> when night and moon join magic made.

Quickly withdraw the blade from the soil, clean it off with a cotton cloth, and put it away until needed.

The Chalice

As previously mentioned the chalice is traditionally made of silver and is a tool of elemental Water. Some Witches use a chalice made of brass, pewter, wood, or polished stone, although such materials are not ideal.

Silver is the metal of the moon, and the chalice represents the womb of the moon goddess. A silver chalice helps the Witch retain the mystical connection for ritual and magical work. On certain occasions the chalice will be used to contain wine. When not using a silver chalice, the inside of the cup area must be coated with a substance that will not react to the wine. In addition a chalice made of any substance should be thoroughly cleaned after use to avoid a buildup of stain.

The chalice can be prepared for use by sprinkling it with some salted water, and then passing it three times through some incense smoke. Then it should be set out beneath the full moon at midnight for one hour. This is best performed when the moon is in the sign of Cancer, Pisces, or Scorpio. These are the water signs of the Zodiac and are traditionally associated with the moon, psychic phenomena, and magic.

Once the chalice has been purified and blessed by moonlight, it can then be dedicated to the service of the Goddess and the God. The Witch dabs the chalice three times with camphor on the outer rim of the cup, which is then traced along the edge with a finger (completing one full circling in a clockwise fashion). While tracing the rim, the Witch recites:

> Witches' cup and womb of power,
> Open now in this shadowed hour.
> Birth each desire, call, and wish,
> In the name of the God and of the Goddess.

In addition to the traditional four tools associated with Witchcraft, we also find several other items used in the Witches' Craft. Some Witches refer to these as the secondary tools of Witchcraft.

These secondary tools are the cauldron, broom, cloak, and ring. Each of them has a practical use as well as a mystical connection. Like most things in Witchcraft, the physical reflects the metaphysical, which itself reflects the spiritual source of all things.

The Cauldron

The Witch's cauldron is featured prominently in fairy tales, legends, myth, and modern movies. Here its use and purpose is typically distorted in order to serve the needs, desires, and agenda of the writer. As noted in chapter two, the Witches' cauldron is a very different thing from the popularized image of a vessel for brewing poisons and magical elixirs made from horrible elements.

In Witchcraft the cauldron is a life-giving vessel of birth and renewal. The cauldron is the seed receiver, and the womb that transforms the potential into the manifest. In ritual and magic, the cauldron represents not only the womb gate, but also the portal to and from the Underworld.

Most Witches will have at least two cauldrons, a small and a large one. The small cauldron is filled halfway with sand, upon which a small charcoal block can be placed. This cauldron is used to burn incense, ritual debris, or pieces of parchment used in spell casting. The large cauldron is used for ritual purposes and major works of magic. See chapter ten for more information.

The Broom

Like the cauldron, there is a distorted image of the broom's purpose and use. Naturally the broom does not allow the Witch to fly through the sky in the material realm. However, one of its oldest uses was to banish spirits that gathered in the air and in the wind.

Traditionally the Witch's broom is comprised of an ash branch with birch twigs bound together by willow straps at one end. In old folk-magic beliefs, birch had the power to bar spirits from entering the world of the living and to banish spirits that gathered on low tree branches and in the open rafters of houses. One belief held that by thrashing the air with the bristle end of the broom, the spirits were forced to flee from the birch.

In some Traditions of Witchcraft the broom is used to sweep the ritual area prior to casting the gathering circle. This purifies the setting on both the material and spiritual level. Some Witches use the broom as a "barred door," placing it sideways at the circle's edge where participants will enter and exit the circle.

The symbolism of the broom extends into the other woods that are used to construct the tool. As noted in chapter two, the ash tree is associated with the sea. Hecate, one of the primary goddesses of Witchcraft, was given a portion of the sea, the earth and sky by Zeus, the king of the gods. In old European lore the willow tree is sacred to Hecate, and is associated with the Underworld. This brings the Witch's broom under the domain of Hecate and makes it a tool that can channel power in the three realms: The Underworld, Middle World, and Overworld.

The Cloak

A hooded cloak is sometimes worn by Witches, evoking a mystical aura. In a ritual setting, wearing a hood pulled up over the head (whether on a cloak or a robe) is a sign of being *in the shadows*, which denotes an immersion into the ancient hidden mysteries. It is, in effect, an outward sign that the Witch has left the mundane personality behind and has donned his or her magical persona.

According to oral tradition, during the days of the Inquisition, Witches used to render themselves unseen in the night by wearing either a black hooded robe or hooded cloak. By wearing the hood pulled down over the face, placing the hands inside the robe/cloak, and squatting down by a tree or bush in the woods, the Witch became invisible to the searchers. This is reportedly the origin of the legend that Witches could vanish into thin air.

As a symbol, the black hooded cloak or robe denotes the Witch as a "child of the night," belonging to the realm of the moon and its goddess. The Witch is, in a very real sense, the mystic who sees in the world the reflections of metaphors that point to the spiritual workings of the creators. This inner mechanism animates and directs the material realm. As human greed continues to provoke the collapse of the ecological equilibrium of the Earth, the Witch as a mystic and a magician is needed now more than ever.

The Ring

Traditionally the Witch wears a ring that bears the essence of magic, which is symbolized by the pentagram. It is, in effect, a sign of the covenant between Nature and the Witch. The pentagram symbolizes the quintessence of the inner mechanism of Nature.

According to ancient teachings, the creation of the Universe occurred when the four basic elements of Earth, Air, Fire, and Water were drawn together in harmony under the direction of divine spirit. This basic theme appears in many ancient myths wherein order arises within chaos. This is sometimes referred to as the "taming of the elements."

The ring of power worn by Witches symbolizes one who possesses the ability to direct the elemental forces, keeping them in harmony through the Witch's rapport with the divine source, for all that a Witch does is first discerned through his or her spiritual connection. This requires a turning inward to the divine spark within, which is given by the divine creators. The divine spark maintains a living connection between the soul and divine consciousness from which it sprang forth.

The ring is a magical tool, but what is magic and how does it work? In the next chapter we will examine how Witches view magic. We shall also explore the realm of magic and discover the inner mechanisms that allow magical energy to be accessed by the Witch. Let us turn and investigate the magical craft of the Witches.

EIGHT

The Magical Craft

When people think about Witchcraft they commonly imagine it to be the practice of magic and spell casting. Indeed, these things are part of what might be called the Witches' craft, along with the making of incense, oils, and herbal potions. However, magic is only a small part of Witchcraft, and might be referred to as a side matter, for Witchcraft is a philosophy first, a religion second, and a magical system third. The three aspects are, however, inseparable.

In Witchcraft, magic is defined as the art of causing one's desires to manifest in accord with one's envisioned will. This is first accomplished through exercises that are designed to strengthen the will and the person's ability to visualize. Picturing clearly in your mind exactly what you want and then focusing your will and determination on achieving it is the foundation of one's magical ability. A popular concept in modern Witchcraft is that if you visualize your desire and believe you will achieve it, then it will manifest. Unfortunately, that is not enough to make your magic consistently successful.

When I used to teach Magic 101 classes in Witchcraft, I utilized a little trick to help people understand the principle of magic. At the beginning of the class I set a closed wooden box on a stand in front of me. Then I asked for a volunteer from the assembled students. Once the volunteer was in place, I asked him or her to come up and take the dollar bill out from inside the box while I continued the class.

The volunteer came up to the box, opened it, and remarked, "But there is no dollar bill inside!" I replied, "Are you sure?" and the helper held up the empty box saying, "Yeah, see!" Next I pretended to look perplexed, and then said, "Well, you know what a dollar bill looks like, right?" The person replied, "Sure, of course I do." Then I said, "So, when I said there was a dollar bill in the box, you saw it in your mind, right?" The volunteer nodded in agreement.

"Well," I continued, "did you believe me when I said there was a dollar in the box?" The volunteer answered, "Yes" and then I once again pretended to look puzzled, replying, "Okay, so let me see if I understand this correctly. You visualized the dollar bill and believed it was in the box, but when you opened the box it was empty." Looking around at the students gathered before me, I said, "So, I guess that visualization and belief are not enough to manifest one's desires. There must be something missing here. Can anyone guess what that might be?"

Everyone tried to avoid eye contact and spent a moment in fear that I would call upon them for the answer. Instead I finally remarked, "Well, the missing ingredient was energy. Neither myself or anyone else made the effort to put the dollar in the box." The expected groan came back from the students, but the point had been made. Without an investment of energy, nothing is going to happen.

The essential formula for magic is that three things are needed in order for manifestation to take place: time, space, and energy. This is sometimes called the triangle of manifestation. The time is when the act is performed, the space is where it takes place, and the energy is the action required (whether it is a ritual performance, ecstatic dancing, or some other method of raising energy). All three elements must be brought together in order for magic to take root and for manifestation to occur.

Capturing the Magic

Another trick I use in order to teach people is what I call "capturing the magic." In Magic 101 classes, I prearrange with the host to have the lights go out and back on as I request in the moment. Then I begin to talk about Witchcraft as a magical system. When I arrive at the point where I define magic, I tell everyone that I want to show him or her something.

I ask the host to turn the lights out, and when it is dark I begin to speak in soft measured tones that are meant to evoke a mystical atmosphere in the room. Then I tell everyone "Okay, in a few moments I'm going to perform an act of magic that you will all experience right here and now." I pause for a few seconds and then continue, "Okay, I will begin now on the count of three" and then I slowly count out loud. After counting to three, I again pause for a few seconds as I stand in the darkness. When I say "All right then . . ." it is the host's cue to turn the lights back on.

There in the light everyone sits blinking and looking around. Some people look puzzled and others look concerned. Then I ask them, "How many people think that nothing happened?" The reactions vary from class to class, but more often than not no one raises a hand. Next I ask, "As you sat there in the darkness, and I said in a few moments I was going to perform an act of magic, wasn't there, even for just a split second, the feeling that literally anything was about to happen? Couldn't you feel it all around you?" The silent nodding of "yes" is always the only reply.

I explained to the students that something indeed had taken place, and that I did as I said I would do. I evoked the potentiality, and for a brief, fleeting moment they had experienced the essence of magic. There in the darkness, in that one brief moment anything and everything was possible. Through this experience the students had captured the magic, or in a very real sense had recaptured the magic that was lost to them when they surrendered childhood and embraced the prefabricated world that others had prepared for them to grow up in.

The Magical State of Mind

If you've ever observed young children at play, then you've readily noted that it takes little more than a cape to make them a superhero in their minds. With a feather headdress a child can fully become an American Indian, or with a cap pistol in a holster the child can become a famous gunslinger. Here a simple tool transforms an open consciousness. This is, in part, what is called the magical consciousness.

Witches use the creation of a magical state of consciousness as part of a training system. The ritual setting itself helps invoke the magical consciousness. This begins with marking out a circle on the ground with chalk, rope, or a ring of stones, which commences the initial stages that eventually culminate in a transformation of the mundane into the mystical. Two candles are lighted and set on the altar, which sits in or near the center of the circle. Candles or torches are placed and lighted at each of the four quarters of the ritual circle.

As the candlelight flickers in the darkness, incense is lighted and smoke begins to rise. It mingles with the soft light of the candles, creating a magical mist. The scent fills the ritual setting and fixes the image of this magical realm firmly in the mind and the senses. Here in this mystical setting the man or woman performing the task now realizes the Witch within, and the magical consciousness emerges.

The laying out of a ritual circle and the setting of an altar helps the Witch to remove herself/himself from the secular world. This is a conscious focus of personal effort designed to transform the setting into sacred space. The glow of candlelight, the movement of shadows, the scent of incense, and the sight of ritual tools all contribute to alter one's state of consciousness.

Once the Witch has achieved the proper magical state of mind, then access to magical energy can be accomplished. The occult principle of "like attracts like" draws the Witch and the magical realm closer together in alignment. Once a harmonious state is achieved, the two may interact with one another. For the Witch anything is now possible, and so he or she then calls to the powers that be.

Magic and the Four Elements

In the beliefs of Witchcraft the basic structure of anything existing within the material and spiritual realm is comprised of one or more of the four elemental natures. Earth is that property which binds and gives form. Air is that property which liberates and stimulates. Fire is that property which animates and activates. Water is that property which makes things mutable and flexible.

According to the teachings, everything in the Universe has a dual nature, and therefore the four elements also possess a duality (what can be termed their negative aspects). In this context, the element of Earth can be rigid, Air flighty, Fire destructive, and Water stagnant. However, through the intervention of Divine Spirit (the so-called fifth element), the four elements are kept in a positive and peaceful state of existence. It is important to understand that when we speak of the Four Elements we are speaking of types of energy. The physical forms of the Four Elements in the material world are manifestations of elemental principles and are not the elements themselves.

Empedocles (a student of the teachings of Pythagoras) was the first person known to have taught the concept of the Four Elements as a single cohesive doctrine. He was also the first person to introduce the concept of the Four Elements into astrology, and their role in discerning the basic nature of the Zodiac signs. He lived around 475 B.C.E. in his native homeland of Sicily, where he presented the teachings concerning the Four Elements as the fourfold root of all things. These are the traditional assignments in European Occultism derived from the teachings of Empedocles:

Earth:	Taurus, Virgo, Capricorn
Air:	Gemini, Libra, Aquarius
Fire:	Aries, Leo, Sagittarius
Water:	Cancer, Scorpio, Pisces

Earth:	cold + dry
Air:	hot + moist
Fire:	hot + dry
Water:	cold + moist

Most occultists credit Philippus Aureolus Paracelsus with what can be called the doctrine of the Four Elements. Paracelsus was an alchemist who taught that the four primary elements consisted of both a vaporous and a tangible substance. He believed that each element existed as both a physical element and a spiritual element. Paracelsus taught that just as there were two types of matter in Nature, physical and etheric, so too must there be two types of Nature (the Physical World and the Supernatural World). He further believed that within the Supernatural World there existed beings native to each of the elemental regions therein. Thus Paracelsus assigned Gnomes to Earth, Sylphs to Air, Salamanders to Fire, and Undines to Water.

During the Middle Ages men and women were believed to have composite natures, meaning they were a blend of spirit, mind, and body. Elemental Beings were considered to be creatures of a single nature related entirely to the property of their corresponding element. Just as fish are creatures of the water, and birds are creatures of the air, each elemental is unique in form and function in a way that is appropriate to its elemental environment.

Paracelsus taught that Elementals were invisible to human sight because they existed in a more subtle state than physical forms or phenomena. It was believed, however, that by condensing the etheric material of their forms, Elementals could appear in the physical world of Nature whenever they pleased. As Paracelsus stated it, the Elementals live in the interior elements while men and women live in the exterior elements.

The Elemental Gateway

While Witches create magical energy in the material realm, magic actually takes root in the astral dimension. The key here is for the Witch to transmit this energy to the astral realm. To accomplish this, the Witch establishes a gateway between the worlds. Once a gateway is opened, the magical energy can then be directed outward. For further information on such techniques, I direct the reader to my previous books, *Wiccan Magick* and *The Witches' Craft*.[1]

Lying just beyond the gateway leading from the ritual circle is the elemental plane of forces. This can be thought of as a circular river flowing to and from the astral dimension. Whatever enters the elemental flow from the material realm is then carried to the astral and vice versa. Whatever takes root in the astral material then manifests in the material world. The trick is getting one's desires to take root in the first place.

In the magical art of Witchcraft, in order for a desire to take root it must have a cohesive energy form. Therefore the Witch creates a "formed thought" that is generated by a strong visual image. Raising energy and directing it into the visual image then vitalizes the image. This is a simultaneous act and requires a careful and strong focus. Once the energy is released, the thought-form is then bound with one or more of the four elements. This would be whichever element (by its unique character) matches the nature of the desire.

Daydreams, fantasies, and musings raise energy but lack any substantial cohesion (unless they become obsessive). Therefore they cannot take root on the astral plane and become manifest in the material realm. Instead, in some cases, their forms can attach themselves to the aura of the person generating them. If this happens, the person can find himself or herself living in a dreamworld, rather than fully participating in a practical course concerning his or her own life.

Because creating viable thought-forms requires creativity and energy, Witches evoke elemental spirits to their ritual circles to aid in the formation of magic. The elementals are asked to impart their nature to the magic or spell being created. With their assistance the Witch can direct more energy into the creation of magic than she can or he can alone as a single individual. A coven of Witches can be even more successful in this regard.

Magic and the Witches' Tools

In the art of magic (from the perspective of Witchcraft) the pentacle, wand, athame, and chalice are the material links to the elemental energies they represent. In one sense they are bridges to the elemental realm across which the magician extends his or her consciousness and willpower. To utilize any of the tools is to wield the power of the element connected to it, for an element tool is, in part, a tangible metaphor for the metaphysical nature it symbolizes.

The Witch and the tool must "meet" in the elemental nature itself. This can be accomplished by one of two means. Traditionally each tool was acquired by directly encountering the element to which it was assigned. This required the initiate to literally "brave the elements" in order for him or her to obtain a ritual tool. For example, the wand might be suspended from the branch of a tall tree or tied to a rock on a cliff, and the Witch had to climb for the tool. The athame might be set in the center of a large circle of flames, the chalice in a deep pool, and the pentacle deep within a dark cave.

In modern times there is a safer way preferred by many Witches. This simply requires what is called "merging" with the tool. The Witch sits comfortably and holds the tool in his or her hands. Then the Witch pictures herself/himself as a hollow vessel completely surrounded in all directions by one of the four elements. If working with Earth, for example, the Witch would visualize grains of sand pouring into his or her body from the top of the head down to the feet, completely filling the entire body. As the Earth pours in, the Witch imagines the sensation of the element, which in the case of Earth might be heaviness or solidity.

When the element has filled the Witch completely, then he or she exhales the elemental substance out upon the tool, using three long, deep exhalations. During each exhalation the Witch visualizes the elemental substance rushing out of the body from head to toe and into the ritual tool. This basic formula is repeated for each of the elements and each of the tools associated with them. To recap, the pentacle is Earth, wand is Air, athame is Fire, and the chalice is Water.

Having performed the exercise, both the Witch and the tool now share the same relationship to the elemental nature. When the Witch then holds one of the tools, the element is alive and can be invoked or evoked as desired. The elemental spirits sense the vital essence of their elemental nature within the tool (and within the Witch) and are attracted to the display and use of the tool.

It is customary in Witchcraft to never touch or handle another's tools without first asking permission. This is because each tool is intimately linked to the Witch. Some Witches never allow their tools to be touched by anyone, and some Witches will grant permission if protocol is observed.

Traditionally the tools are recharged and blessed again beneath the full moon each month. During the course of a year, this permeates the tool with the energy of the moon in each of the Zodiac signs. The simplest method is to sprinkle the tool with clean spring water and set it out beneath the full moon at midnight for one hour. The tool is then retrieved, dried with a cotton cloth, wrapped in silk, and put away in a dark place at least until after sunset the next day. Silk will not draw energy from the tool, and this helps the energy to "set" within the tool.

Basic Formula of Magic

There are five essential aspects that contribute to the creation of consistently successful works of magic. These aspects are as follows:

1. Personal Will

2. Timing

3. Imagery

4. Direction

5. Balance

One's "personal will" can be thought of as motivation, desire, or persuasiveness. The Witch must invest the "raised power" of his or her personal interest in the outcome of the goal in order to provide enough energy to initiate the process of magical manifestation. The stronger the emotional investment, the more power that can be raised. However, the sense of "need" and "longing" must be suppressed when working magic, as such feelings prevent the full release of power toward the desired goal.

A mundane example of this principle is known to many gamblers. If you need to win because you need the money, you won't win. If you don't care about the money, you have a chance of winning. Therefore, the sense of need and longing must be suppressed, and the will must be focused only upon a detached view of the desired outcome.

In December, 2002, a man in West Virginia won $360 million dollars in a lotto drawing. He was already a multimillionaire with earnings of $17 million a year. He bought one single ticket and most likely gave the matter no further thought, because he didn't need the money. Elsewhere in the state, hundreds of people who desperately needed the money spent funds they could not afford and bought multiple tickets. They prayed to win and probably thought about little else from the time they purchased the ticket until the winner was announced.

From a magical perspective, no energy was released toward their goal. All of the energy literally stayed with them and swirled in their bellies and hearts. In a sense, the winner actually won by default because his lack of concern left him open and receptive.

Timing is also important in the performance of magic and can mean success or failure. The best time to release and direct magic is when the target is most receptive. Receptivity is usually assured when the target is passive rather than active. The waxing or waning phase of the moon must also be taken into account, as well as the season of the year. Working in harmony with the natural flow of energy will assist it. Working against the natural flow will resist a successful manifestation.

Imagery is essential to magic and the success of any work depends partly upon images created by the mind. This is where the imagination enters into the formula, for anything that serves to intensify the emotions will ultimately contribute to success.

Even a drawing, photo, or illustration can help the Witch link with his or her desire, for imagery can serve as a guiding device in its role as a representation of the desired outcome.

Once sufficient energy has been raised, the Witch must direct it toward the desired manifestation—but, as noted earlier, any feelings of anxiety concerning the results will only serve to retain the energy. Likewise each time the mind turns to thinking about the outcome, the energy draws the images and concepts back and away from the goal. For consistent success, the matter must be given no further thought once a work of magic is completed.

The last aspect of magic is related to personal balance. The Witch must weigh the need for working magic against the consequences of achieving the goal, taking into consideration the target of the desire as well as the Witch's own personal well-being. Anger, greed, lust, and revenge are types of energy that can and will have repercussions for all concerned. Instead, the seasoned Witch seeks an inward balance of emotion and reason before casting a spell or performing an act of magic.

Another aspect of balance concerns the exterior world. A Witch has power with Nature, not over Nature. Therefore the Witch does not seek to disturb or upset the natural flow of things without good cause. The seasoned Witch does not attempt to make rain when the weather is clear and dry, nor does the Witch try to make plants grow in the snow, and so forth. The Witch works with the seasons and the cycles of Nature in order to achieve her or his magical desires.

The Witches' Pyramid

The Witches' Pyramid is a concept that depicts the necessary components that contribute to achieving the manifestation of one's magical desire. The pyramid is comprised of these sides marked with the attributes:

- Personal Will

- Imagination

- Visualization

(In the center of the pyramid lies the expectation of success.)

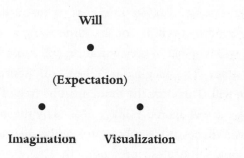

Will

●

(Expectation)

●   ●

Imagination   **Visualization**

Expectation is essential to a successful manifestation. The Witch must will a thing to be, imagine the outcome in her/his mind, and visualize what is desired. Beyond this, the Witch must have the expectation that it will manifest in complete accord with the desire.

Imagination is an important component in creating magical effects. People who do not possess knowledge of how magic works, nor have any experience with it, may feel that imagination is purely a fantasy. To the Witch, however, imagination is a vaporous quality that can condense thoughts into formed images. On the Physical Plane, a person's thoughts (through imagination) can manifest as a novel, a movie, or a work of art. On the Astral Plane, a person's imagination can manifest energy images that are as real to astral entities as any physical form is to material beings.

Consistently effective magic requires the actions of both the imagination and the personal will. The will by itself is an undefined current of energy. The imagination by itself lacks vitality. When the two factors are brought together, substantial magical effects are possible. In practical application, the Witch must first activate the imagination so that an image of the desired effect is created. Then the personal will must be used to direct the energy of the imagination.

In Witchcraft, imagination can be likened to the womb, and in this context the will becomes the impregnating seed. When joined together they can produce the "magical child," which is the *desire* made manifest. In the art of magic it is important to understand that will is not the same thing as desire. The personal will is an act of concentration and must be kept separate from desire. The imagination arises from desire and is vitalized by the will. Therefore the mind must be free of desire when focusing the will upon the image evoked by the imagination. This is why Witches use symbols and sigils—because they are unemotional substitutes representing the desire, goal, and manifestation. In effect, they help free the Witch from attachment.

Magickal Links

It is very old folk-magic belief that anything connected with a person contains an energy link with that person. For example, a person's hair holds the vibrations of his or her energy pattern. Therefore by the use of sympathetic magic that person can be influenced by energy directed to him or her. Sympathetic magic is a concept in which one object can affect another object that contains a direct link. This is the basic notion of the so-called voodoo doll, which in Witchcraft is called a poppet.

In sympathetic magic, hair can serve as a point of concentration and as a kind of "homing device" for the directed energy. The same is true for unwashed items of clothing and other personal items. By making an image of an individual and placing his or her personal items within it, one creates a center of focus that is magically connected to the individual. Through this method the Witch can perform healing and other acts of folk magic from a distance.

In Witchcraft it is believed that everything is linked together and is essentially inseparable. This can be visualized as a giant spider's web with each joint on a strand being a physical object, person, place, or situation in the material plane. The movement, disturbance, or breakage of any thread causes a ripple that passes a vibration to everything on the web. In this sense everything can be reached and influenced by connecting with the strands of the web. This is part of the Witches' magical Craft.

Witches have been called the weavers and shapers of magic. They use the elemental substance of creation itself to work their magic. Theirs is the world of the mysteries, a place between the worlds. The Witch moves between the magical and natural world at will and is equally at home in both realms. For the Witch, magic is simply part of life and it permeates all that a Witch does.

The Hidden Doorway

It is in the understanding that all things are linked together that the Witch realizes the inner mechanism of the Otherworld. Here the secret mysteries reside and are shielded by the guardian mind. The guardian mind is that part of our consciousness that sees the world in a practical and linear manner. It examines, analyzes, and categorizes everything we experience. Another name for the guardian mind is the conscious mind.

Several years ago I was presiding over a ritual, and in attendance was a young, first-degree Witch. It was the first time for her to participate in a full ritual working, and she was very excited. The weather prevented us from being outside this night, and so we decided to hold the ritual indoors. Everything went well and eventually the time came to complete the ritual.

When all was done, we extinguished the candles and one of the initiates stumbled off into darkness trying to find the light switch. In the meantime the new initiate moved to my side and commented "It was really *cool* how your amulet was reflecting light during the ritual." Just as she finished her words, the lights came on, she looked at my chest, and then meekly remarked, "Umm . . . you're not wearing an amulet." I replied, "No, not tonight," and I went to work cleaning up the surface of the altar.

After a few moments the initiate spoke again, "Well, maybe one of the candle flames reflected off the blade of the athame on the altar and the light was shining on you." I replied, "Yeah, that's probably what it was," and I continued to put away the ritual items. A few more moments passed, and the initiate suggested, "Um, maybe what it was, was the street light was coming in through the venetian blinds and caught your chest as you moved in front of the altar." Again I responded, "Yeah, that's probably what it was."

With the ritual behind us, we all settled into the living room and began to chat, drink wine, and enjoy each other's company. As the night wore on, the initiate approached me an additional three times with other various scenarios as to how and why a glow appeared on my chest during the ritual. Needless to say, her guardian mind was well at work.

Just before everyone began to leave for home, she approached me once again. I stopped her, gently placed my hands on her shoulders, and looked her directly in the eyes. "Do you know what you're doing?" I asked. The initiate replied, "What do you mean?" I gave her a teasing shake and said, "You're losing the magic!"

I told her that I didn't know what the glow on my chest had been, and that it could have been anything. I explained that by seeking mundane explanations she had robbed herself of the essence of magic and the potential of the moment. Then I suggested that in the future she should simply be present in the moment during a ritual and not try to analyze things, but simply experience them. There will always be time later in the night to reflect back and discern what took place (and what did not).

The subconscious mind perceives things very differently than does the conscious mind. For example, in a dream, if you are driving a car and it suddenly becomes a bicycle, you just start pedaling. If, in a dream, you find yourself standing at a street corner and a bus pulls up and opens the doors, you get on the bus even though you don't know where you're going or why. If any of these events happened in the mundane world, for the conscious mind there would be serious questions requiring an answer.

To the subconscious mind the car, the bicycle, and the bus are only symbols of concepts. To the subconscious mind it is the journey itself that is the focus of the dream and not the related vehicles. The subconscious mind is conceptual (seeing the whole view) while the conscious mind is detail oriented (focusing largely on the components). This is why the conscious mind can reject the concept of magic, while the subconscious mind readily accepts it as a fact.

For the Witch, part of working magic requires getting past the guardian and accessing the subconscious levels. The subconscious mind is directly linked to the dreamworld, which is a doorway to the Astral Plane. This is where magical energy takes root and moves toward manifestation. Old legends about secret passwords that open doorways, as well as tales of secret passages through tree trunks and boulders, are all metaphors for getting past the guardian mind in order to enter the hidden realm.

In order to bypass the guardian mind, the Witch must achieve an altered state of consciousness similar to the dream-mind, which accepts whatever is happening and simply responds to it. One of the ways this can be accomplished for the beginner is to use the altar setting as a catalyst. This allows for a gradual awakening of the magical mind.

To awaken the magical mind it is always helpful to extinguish all artificial lights. The guardian mind views night as the time to relax control and prepare for eventual sleep, and therefore the darkness is an aid to slipping past the guardian. Lighting a few candles creates an "otherworld" atmosphere, which is helpful in allowing one to "shake off" the mundane world. Additionally, the flickering flames awaken the primal memory of sitting around the fire-ring beneath the forest canopy, echoes of a time when we lived in harmony with our environment.

Lighting some incense and watching the smoke rise and drift into the air can invoke a sense of the mystical as well. The Witch must mentally enter fully into the moment and allow the consciousness to give way and embrace the notion of magic. If each act is performed with slow and deliberate, focused attention, and with an air of reverence, then the guardian mind becomes hypnotized. This state allows the subconscious mind to awaken and create the dreamworld/astral connections for the Witch.

By placing the elemental tools (pentacle, wand, athame, chalice) on the altar and focusing on their elemental natures, the subconscious mind can then acknowledge their connections to the astral operations. This makes the power and purpose of the tools real within the consciousness of the Witch. Here the props become the metaphors for the principles they represent. Once everything is thus translated and interpreted by the subconscious mind, the Witch can then wield the power of the concept through the use of each tool. Just as in the case of the earlier dream example where the car became a bicycle, in magic the subconscious mind has no argument with the ability of a wand to produce magical effects.

Now that we have explored the magical consciousness of the Witch, let us turn to the next chapter and explore the mysteries that are part of the Witches' world. Here we shall encounter the Otherworld and come to an understanding of mystical views in the religion of Witchcraft.

NINE

The Three Great Mysteries

The ancient Greek writer Hesiod wrote in his work, *The Theogony*, that there are three great mysteries in the life of humankind: *birth, life,* and *death.* The mysteries spoken of by Hesiod point to the questions humans have asked themselves since the beginning: Where did we come from, why are we here, and what happens after we die?[1]

In modern Witchcraft we find a popular passage that refers to a triplex mystery. The verse reads:

> . . . for there be three great mysteries in the life of man, and magic controls them all. To fulfill love, you must return again at the same time and at the same place as the loved ones; and you must meet, know, and remember, and love them again. But to be reborn, you must die, and be made ready for a new body. And to die,

you must be born; and without love, you may not be born.[2]

Gerald Gardner, in his book *Witchcraft Today*, published a slightly different version with the words: "For there are three great events in the life of man—love, death and resurrection in the new body—and magic controls them all."[3]

Almost half a century earlier than the writings of Gerald Gardner, we find those of Charles Leland, who wrote on a similar topic in his book *Etruscan Roman Remains*. In chapter ten, Leland discusses the theme of Witches being born again within their own bloodlines. Here Leland writes:

> There is a rather obscure esoteric doctrine, known in Witch families but not much talked about. A child is born, when, after due family consultation, some very old and wise strega detects in it a long-departed grandfather by his smile, features, or expression.[4]

In the introduction Leland notes that "sorcerers and witches are sometimes born again in their descendants."

Leland goes on to discuss "witch families who cling together and intermarry," which increases the likelihood of a former family Witch returning to be born in his or her lineage. Leland states that by being reborn the Witch grows more powerful each time. According to Leland, the Witch moves on eventually and becomes a powerful spirit.

Central to the theme of the mysteries, as described in both Gardner's and Leland's writings, is the cycle of birth, death, and rebirth. This implies that birth is a doorway to the material world, one that can be entered many times. Each lifetime is an opportunity to gain experience and to hone one's skills. Death is an exit from the material world back into the spirit world. From there the entire process can take place again, allowing the evolution and maturity of the soul to take place over many lifetimes. In Witchcraft we do not find the belief that each person has one lifetime, and that afterward his or her eternal condition is based upon that one-time shot.

In order to understand the three great mysteries, we must explore the concepts underlying each one. Once we possess this basic overview we can then integrate the various elements into a meaningful whole. This is essentially the purpose of a Mystery Tradition, to uncover what lies behind the outer form of expression, for it is the inner mechanism that holds the secrets to the Universe.

Birth

In the ancient mystery systems the cauldron symbolized birth. One of its primary roles was to represent the womb of the Great Mother for ritual and magical purposes. As noted in chapter two, the cauldron is the vessel of transformation. Here begins the process of the soul entering into the material dimension where it interfaces with a new body of flesh.

From the ancient perspective, everything originated in the Underworld. The sun and moon arose from the Underworld, crossed over the world of the living and then descended back into the dark realm below. The Underworld was where the sun and moon "lived." They only briefly visited the world of humankind, for the sun and moon were at home in the darkness. Here is reflected the teaching that light resides in darkness.

When we are in despair, face a serious dilemma, or have to deal with emotional pain, we go inward to the center of our being. It is here, alone with our thoughts, that we enter the darkness of our own Underworld and find the answers, solve the puzzles, and gain personal enlightenment. This is the cauldron within us, and it grants us transformation, release, and rebirth.

It is an old occult teaching that souls awaiting rebirth reside in the moon, which of course is a metaphor for an astral realm. According to the ancient teachings, the sun (as it crosses the sky each day) collects the souls of all who died during the night. The souls are then delivered into the Underworld at sunset. In some Traditions of Witchcraft we find the mythos of the God gathering the souls of the departed and escorting them to the Goddess, into whose care the souls are given.

An ancient belief held that in the Underworld the souls are drawn into the moon. As the moon fills with souls, its light increases until it is a full moon. As the souls are reborn back into the material world, the light of the moon diminishes until it is totally dark and unseen for three days. Plutarch held a similar view when he wrote that souls "resolve" into the moon just as bodies do into the earth, for the moon is of their element. According to Peter Kingsley, in his book *Ancient Philosophy, Mystery, and Magic*, both Plato and Pythagoras alluded to souls living in the moon in various writings (Plato's Phaedo myth being one example).

In an occult sense, the moon is a metaphor for the astral plane. The astral plane is a nonphysical dimension connected to the physical dimension by the elemental plane. The material of the astral plane can be shaped and molded by the energy of "formed-thoughts" projected into its substance. The astral material will mold itself in accord with the formed-thought and take on the shape and represented intent. This can be pictured as melted wax in a bowl forming around any object that is dipped into the wax.

Once the soul enters into the astral substance, a body of energy is formed around it. The shape, condition, nature, and character of the soul dictate what vessel will contain the soul in the next life. The energy of the most recent life is very potent and therefore very influential in determining what type of body and mind the soul will work with in the next life.

According to the old occult teachings, while the soul awaits rebirth it receives an overview of the life to come, highlighted by the major events to come. These include who the parents will be and the result of that experience. Other events such as whether one will marry, have children, experience serious hardships, be successful, and so forth are also indicated. However, free will is not forsaken and the soul may or may not achieve the goal of each life experience (depending upon one's actions or lack thereof).

In the mystery tradition it is said that prior to rebirth the soul is presented with what some call the "soul contract." This essentially sets forth what the soul is to accomplish during any given physical life experience. For as the saying goes: "We are spiritual beings having a human experience, and not human beings having a spiritual experience."

Predestination is not a teaching in Witchcraft because it conflicts with the concept of free will. Some people may argue that the Witches' art of foretelling the future contradicts such a statement. However, divination itself is simply the seeing of patterns established within the astral plane, which will manifest if nothing alters the course. The advantage of being able to predict events is that it allows an individual to avert an outcome or fully embrace its arrival.

In the mystery tradition the future experience of the departing soul can be aided by the living through ritual energy. In other religions, prayers (which are thoughts empowered by emotional energy) are offered for the well-being of the departed soul. The outpouring of positive energy is absorbed into the astral substance, and strengthens those qualities harmonious to the condition of the soul receiving them.

The ancient teachings tell us that a soul awaiting rebirth is drawn from the astral plane by a whirlpool of energy that forms as a result of sexual union on the material plane. In other words, when a couple engages in sexual intercourse an energy vortex is formed around them. The vortex vibrates in harmony with the composite auras of the couple. Souls whose spiritual vibrations are in harmony with the energy of the vortex are then drawn down into the composite aura of the couple. If conception takes place, then the soul is bound to the womb and released from the astral plane.

Life

In the ancient mysteries systems the pentagram symbolized the quintessence of life. The pentagram represents the principle of creation, the four elements of Earth, Air, Fire, and Water brought into balance by the harmony of spirit. The uppermost point of the pentagram represents Spirit, each of the four lower points represent a specific element, and the circle symbolizes the balance and harmony resulting in the principle.

Creativity is one of the key aspects of the life experience. Our ability to create is derived from the divine spark of our creator that dwells within us. To understand this better let us think about the artist and his or her creation. As noted earlier in this book, when an artist carves or shapes a statue, or paints a picture, something of the nature of the artist goes into it. In other words we can say that art reflects the artist, revealing the artist's passion (or lack thereof) and sense of style, symmetry, line, and so forth. By examining and studying a work of art, one can learn something about the artist. The same can be said by studying nature, and here we can learn and discern something about the creators.

If we accept that our creators brought our souls into existence, then we too must bear the mark of that which created us. Within us, at the core, is the divine spark of the creators. Something of the nature of the gods dwells within our souls. By aligning with this connection to the Source, we too can create on a vast scale. The pentagram, as our symbol, is a reminder that we are the spirit at the tip of the star, and we can draw the elements into harmony and thereby create whatever we envision.

Because we have free will, we also have the ability to alter the course of our lives. This is both a gift and a burden because we can make choices that can change the achievement of the goal within our soul contact. Therefore the Witch strives to obtain balance in his or her life, and through a balanced view make the decisions that affect his or her life.

It is an old teaching that the powers of a Witch are strengthened and maintained through an unbroken participation in the eight Sabbats of the year, as well as the full moon rites of each month. It is taught that through such participation a Witch is bathed in the energy inherent at these times of power. The accumulative effect results in the alignment of the chakra centers and the aura to the patterns of Nature. Once the Witch resonates with the current of Nature, then random occurrence is eliminated from the life of the Witch.

Random occurrence falls into the category of accidental. Nothing is accidental in Nature because every event in Nature has a cause and effect relationship. Therefore, becoming more like Nature through alignment brings the events of one's life into the same pattern or set of laws. Once a Witch lives in accord with the Old Ways, the Witch can then look at his or her life and understand (through reflection) that everything he or she is experiencing is a result of personal choices or lack of choices. The Witch is never a victim of life; a Witch is a full participant in his or her life.

It is important to understand that the Source of All Things, or let's use the term "the Universe," does not reward or punish. What the Universe does is to watch, listen, and respond. Whatever we tell it through our thoughts and our actions, it then empowers with an outpouring of matched energy. Therefore, if we dwell on what we don't have or don't want, it simply gives us more of the same lack. In a certain sense, it believes that if we are expending so much energy and time focused on such and such, then we must want whatever we are dwelling upon. Why else would we give it so much attention?

Naturally the reverse is true as well, and if we spend time focusing on what we want to achieve, then the Universe moves energy into the manifestation of that as well. A friend of mine once commented that he had long lived his life saying how he could never afford anything. This continued to be his financial truth until one day he changed his wording to "Okay, so how can I afford" such and such? The Universe responded to the new energy and he moved forward in life with the momentum of positive affirmations.

The Witch knows that magic is present everywhere and in everything. Magic is the energy of potentiality, and it can be filled and shaped with one's thoughts. Once filled (and therefore charged with energy), magic must be directed toward a goal. This can happen equally on a subconscious level as well as on a conscious level. Therefore, it is always important to release magical energy with positive and creative intents instead of negative and restrictive ones.

Armed with the knowledge of magic, the Witch must then turn to discovering his or her purpose in the current life, and his or her place in the scheme of things. This discernment is made through rapport with spirit guides and one's deities. In some traditions this is called finding one's true will and accomplishing it.

In occult tradition the stages of a person's life are divided into four quarters representing Spring, Summer, Fall, and Winter. Each quarter, which is comprised of twenty-one years, begins on the Spring Equinox of the first year and ends on the Winter Solstice of the last year. These are, in effect, the seasons of one's life. The Spring season spans the first year of birth through the twenty-first year. The Summer season encompasses years twenty-two through forty-two. The Autumn season embraces years forty-three through sixty-three. The Winter season encircles years sixty-four through eighty-four.

Death

In the ancient mysteries systems the spiral symbolized death. The spiral is an ancient symbol indicating a doorway between the worlds. In many ways the spiral not only denotes a doorway but also the process of transformation itself. The snake-like image of the spiral suggests that death is a "shedding" of one's skin in preparation for growth and renewal.

In some of the older Witchcraft sects, small spirals were painted upon the dead with menstrual blood. This was meant to connect them with the womb and the blood of rebirth/renewal. The blood was also intended to magically draw the dead back to be reborn among their own clan. This, of course, is the basis of the concept in Witchcraft of returning to life through one's ancestral line.

Early burial customs involved placing the body in the branches of trees (see chapter two). At a later period in time, bodies were placed in caves. Eventually bodies were placed atop stacked branches and burned in an act of cremation. This made the connection back to the primal purifying fire of Vesta and the sacred tree with its connection to deity and to the Underworld. With the flesh quickly returned to the elements, the soul was free to enter into the Otherworld.

It is a belief in many Witchcraft traditions that when a person dies his or her soul crosses over into a realm that many Witches call the Summerland. This is an astral realm envisioned as a place of eternal summer. Here the soul rests, is renewed, and then prepares for the rebirth experience. Legends regarding the Summerland speak of meadows and rolling hills, with forests, rivers, lakes, and streams. Here dwell all the mythological creatures of Paganism such as unicorns, dragons, centaurs, satyrs, nymphs, and so forth. This is due to the thought-forms that have manifested in response to centuries of visualization, belief, and storytelling.

From an occult perspective, a soul would experience the Summerland in accord with his or her personal vision of it. The overall experience, however, would be modified by what many modern Witches call Karma. From an occult perspective a releasing or burning-off of negative energy accumulated during each life experience must take place in order for the soul to progress. This prepares the soul for a new and less "tainted" life experience to come.

In cases where a person has performed great wrongs (for example, a Hitler figure), the Karmic energies still adhere to the soul and create significant challenges in the next life or even several lifetimes to come. These challenges are designed to allow the soul an opportunity to be cleansed and healed, although the average person will often regard them as hardships. It seems reasonable that if we were meant to readily recall our past lives we all would do so naturally. Since this is not the case, it suggests that not knowing is part of the purification by fire process.

The Three Planes of Existence

Early references to the existence of three realms that comprise the Universe appear among the ancient Greeks. Hesiod wrote in his *Theogony* of three realms called Chaos, Gaea, and Eros. From these realms the earth issued forth, as did the heavens and the Underworld. Hesiod describes the inescapable lot of humankind assigned to interplay of the gods and Cosmic Forces. He also outlines the ways that humankind can progress through a series of guidelines he sets forth.

It is noteworthy that Hesiod directs the teachings toward farmers, which suggests a relationship with Nature. Hesiod counsels people to be observant of Nature and to live in accord with her. He cautions:

Let not the gray spring go by unnoticed in her time,
nor the rain in its season. Walk past the blacksmith's

shop in winter where crowds gather at his fire for warmth and gossip. For this keeps a man from his work. Winter can be a harsh time of hopelessness, let it not catch you in need.[6]

At later periods following the time of Hesiod, ancient Greek philosophers wrote about four mystical realms. One popular theory envisioned them as four worlds through which the soul must pass. The first realm was the material world, where the soul dwelled in a body of flesh and bone. Following the death of the physical body, the soul then passed into a lunar realm. Here it took on a body of moonlight, a type of spectral or ghost-like body. As was the case in the material world, the moon-body eventually died also, and crossed over in the realm of the sun world.

In the realm of the sun, the soul entered into a body of etheric fire, the so-called sun body. This fire forged the entire soul in preparation for the final body that awaited it in the next and last realm. Once the sun body died, the soul then entered into the realm of the starry heavens. Here it took on a stellar body of light and then passed into one of the heaven worlds that was in harmony with the spirit of the soul. In the stellar realm the soul existed for eternity, dwelling in a community of souls.

In the Celtic religion, the Druids reportedly taught the concept of a three-realm Universe, which was often depicted in the image of three concentric circles. These realms were called Annwn, Abred, and Gwynvyd. Annwn (the Welsh Underworld) is depicted as "the primal cauldron of form" from which all life issues forth into Abred (see p. 148). In Abred each soul experiences life in all physical forms, from lowest to highest. Once a soul reaches human form, it has the opportunity to enter the realm of Gwynvyd, which is the so-called heaven world. If it falls short of attaining Gwynvyd, the soul falls back into rebirth within Abred. If it succeeds, the soul then works its way up through a series of higher worlds within the realm of Gwynvyd.

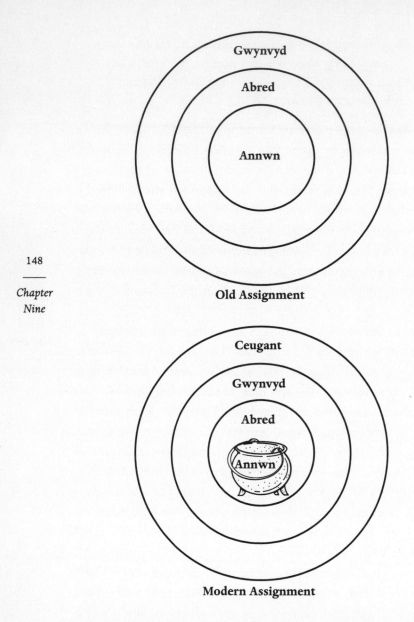

Old Assignment

Modern Assignment

Surrounding the three realms is the sphere of Ceugant, which is the realm of divinity where only the deity can dwell.

Currently a disagreement exists concerning the assignment of the Celtic realms. An old work known as the *Barddas* depicts Abred in the center circle surrounded by Gwynvyd, which is then encircled by Ceugant. Annwn is absent from the arrangement as a separate realm. The *Book of Dwyfyddiaeth* (from the same era as the Barddas) contains a conflicting passage regarding the order of the realms. It suggests that Abred and Annwn are two separate realms, then lists Gwynvyd but does not include Ceugant.[6] This has created some confusion concerning the Celtic view of the planes.

Most modern commentators attempt to rectify the order by placing Annwn in the Circle of Abred (the earth-plane where souls work off the impurity that is attached to them). The Circle of Gwynvyd is then next in order and is envisioned as a place where "justified" spirits reside, the so-called realm of heaven. Then surrounding Gwynvyd is placed the circle of Ceugant.

In the revised order, Annwn sits at the base of Abred and generates souls into the world of the living. In Abred these souls reincarnate many times until they obtain a purified state that renders them suitable to enter Gwynvyd. In the modern view, Gwynvyd becomes a realm of levels that the soul passes through in a process that further purifies it and makes it suitable to enter Ceugant. Ceugant is then depicted as the Heavenworld where one is united with the Source.

In the older texts, Annwn is the abode of those souls who cannot enter either Abred or Gwynvyd. This suggests that their spiritual condition binds them to this realm, but the time period involved seems absent in Celtic literary sources. However, as the older writings indicate that souls may reincarnate from Annwn into Abred, the length of time does not appear to be eternal.

In the text of the Barddas we find a set of teachings setting forth guidelines for the progression of the soul. According to the teachings, humans are subject to suffering, change, and choice. Men and women may attach themselves to objects and situations in the physical plane, or may liberate themselves from these things as they choose. This implies that it is attachment itself that causes the soul to return to Abred.

In the realm of Gwynvyd the soul passes into a state of forgetfulness, which removes the chance recurrence of attachment to the realm of Abred through recall of a former life. In Gwynvyd there is said to be no recollection of sorrow. In the lower realms of Annwn and Abred, sorrow was necessary in order for the soul to progress and make the needed changes and modifications in life.

According to the old teachings, humans may fall back into Abred many times in their quest for Gwynvyd. This is a purifying process that prepares one for the state of spirituality necessary to remain within the higher dimensions of nonphysical existence. To reach Gwynvyd, one must have experienced all things and shed the limitations that caused attachment within physical existence.

It is also taught that one must retain the knowledge of these former existences. This appears to contradict the concept of the "forgetfulness of sorrow" in Gwynvyd. However, the teaching means that one remembers without the emotional response. In recalling a memory the pain and sorrow it evoked in one's former life is not experienced by the soul's recollection of it.

The Seven Planes of Modern Occultism

Because Witchcraft is a religion that has evolved over the course of time and is still in that process, we find additional concepts drawn from outside sources and cultures. One of the most profound additions is that of Western occultism, which itself has some eclectic elements.

In the Western occult view of the Universe there are seven planes that comprise creation. These are called, in order from highest to lowest, the Ultimate, Divine, Spiritual, Mental, Astral, Elemental, and Material. Each of these exists as a series of vibratory states of existence occupying the same space, and yet functioning as separate realms due to their unique nature.

The Ultimate Plane is what can be called the unknowable realm. It is beyond our comprehension and is essentially the source from which all things issued forth. That it exists and is the source is all that can be said about it, other than that it gave birth to divinity.

The next realm is called the Divine Plane. This is where divinity itself became aware of its own existence. Here is where the archetypes of all gods and goddesses exist. It is the realm of divine consciousness and activity.

The Spiritual Plane follows in order and is the dwelling place of the "beings of light." On this plane highly evolved beings who are no longer bound to the "Wheel of Rebirth" come to abide. Depending upon the religious belief system such beings are often referred to as ascendant masters, spirit guides, angels, archons, and so forth.

The Mental Plane is the realm of pure cohesive images generated from the higher planes (although it can receive images from the lower planes as well, according to the expertise of the Witch). Divine thought pours into the mental realm, which then sends a ripple downward through the lower planes and eventually into the material.

The Astral Plane is where mental images (from above or below) take root in the etheric substance of this realm. The astral substance then surrounds the image and makes it become a form. This can be likened to spray painting a clear crystal object, for example, a statue of a horse. The paint brings out the detail of the image and gives it dimension. Whatever successfully takes root on the astral plane will eventually manifest on the physical dimension.

The Elemental Plane (also known as the plane of forces) carries energy imprints to and from the astral plane. Images that have successfully formed in the astral material are drawn by magnetism into the elemental stream, which brings the image into the material world. Everything from a chair that you sit in to this book you are reading was once only an image of its creator.

The Material Plane is the lowest vibratory dimension of the seven planes. Its vibration is so low that things become seemingly solid on the material dimension. This book, for example, feels like a solid object, but in reality it is a mass of atoms bound together by chemical energy. Between each atom there is a space, therefore technically the book is not really a solid object. From an occult perspective the material world is an illusion that binds things together into appearances. For the Witch it is clear that outer form shields the inner truth from the physical senses.

Now that we have explored the Three Great Mysteries and pondered the realms that lie beyond the world of the living, it is time to turn toward the source itself. Let us open the next chapter and closely examine the concept of the God and Goddess, as well as the many spirits who dwell in this world and the next.

TEN

Deities and Spirits

The limitations of the present state of our human condition prevent us from truly knowing and understanding what can be called *The Source of All Things*. As a race we have caught glimpses of it and have tried to capture it in the creation of myths, legends, and lofty theological concepts.

In the history of our race we have worshipped everything from trees to the personification of the Divine in human form. In ancient times the Divine appeared in images called gods and goddesses. Today many people personify the Divine as a singular being called God.

As noted earlier in this book, many modern Witches believe that the Divine Source is comprised of masculine and feminine aspects or polarities. In an attempt to better understand the Divine Source, the polarities are labeled "Goddess" and "God" and each one is further divided into the various aspects and natures attributed to a variety of gods and goddesses. This is designed to reveal a better understanding of the whole by examining its parts.

The deity forms that are found in Witchcraft have evolved from concepts associated with ancient hunter-gatherer societies. To our ancestors the world was a place of mystery and the forces of Nature seemed directed by something conscious. Gods and spirits were believed to be behind the phenomena of storms, earthquakes, seasonal changes, and the cycles of the sun and moon. The heavens in particular, with the clouds, sun, and moon moving about, and the stars filling the night sky, seemed like another realm above the world of humankind.

Many of the early gods were deities associated with mountaintops and with tall trees, both reaching up into the sky. As humans became "civilized," their concepts of divinity began to mature and therefore their deity images did as well. One such example is the mountain god Yahweh who later evolved to become the Jehovah figure, the Hebrew God of the Universe.

The earliest images that appear to suggest deity are birds carved from rock or painted on walls. The oldest of these bird images were female in form and suggested Nature. Perhaps the association of birds with the sky suggested a link to the divine. With the development of mythology, birds begin to appear as the companions and servants of gods and goddesses such as Athena, Odin, Zeus, Bran, Nantosuelta, Badhbh, Macha, Brigid, and a host of others. The earliest bird images of the Neolithic period depicted primarily waterfowl, but later in time the eagle, raven, hawk, crane, goose, and swan become the main characters.

During the hunter-gatherer period of human society, the creatures of the forest took on great symbolic significance. So powerful was the impact of the nature and character of various animals that they featured prominently in fairy tales, legends, and folklore. Even today animal characters play a significant role in many popular movies, particularly those produced by Disney.

The night, and creatures of the night, gave rise to many imaginings for early humans. The so-called supernatural beings that appear in cultural lore were conceived in the darkness of night, and represented both the fears and desires our primitive ancestors held. The moon and the stars, themselves "creatures" of the night, came to be associated with the essence of what was thought to be mystical and supernatural.

The word "moon" is ultimately derived from the Indo-European *me*, which means (among other things) a "quality of mind" as well as a "measurement." The Greek *metis* (wisdom) and the Old High German *muot* (mind or spirit) share the same root word as moon. The word for star in Latin is *astrum*, from which is derived the modern term "astral." Astral literally means star-like, very much like the word asterisk, which means star-shaped and is derived from the Latin *aster* (star).

The moon is known to influence the menstrual cycle of women, which is why the words "menstrual" and "moon" share a relationship with the root word *mensis* (meaning month). There are many relationships between blood, wombs, rebirth, and goddess imagery emerging during the Neolithic period and continuing into later periods, but even as long ago as the Paeleolithic period the symbols of moon, womb, and goddess (in bird form) were connected.

Prehistoric burial sites reveal skeletal remains stained with red ochre, as are the personal items presumed to belong to the dead person. The individuals were buried in a fetal position facing the east quarter, which is where the moon returns from each night. This suggests to the modern mind the theme of death and rebirth connected to blood and the moon. As noted earlier in this book, the moon has long been linked to the souls of the dead and the Underworld.

The ancient Etruscans, a mysterious race that lived in what is now northern Italy, believed that the moon was a living goddess. Some anthropologists, such as the late Marija Gimbutas, believe that the Etruscans were the heirs to the Neolithic religion of Old Europe. There is an abundance of Neolithic art that joins feminine forms with lunar symbols. This has led many people to believe that our Neolithic ancestors worshipped the Goddess in connection with the moon.

The Goddess

The Goddess-form in Witchcraft is associated in symbolism with the moon, the seasons of the year, and the cycles of death and rebirth. In modern Witchcraft the goddess is conceived of as a three-fold goddess comprising the aspects of Maiden, Mother, and Crone. Each of these is marked by a phase of the moon. The waxing crescent symbolizes the Maiden. The full moon represents the Mother and the waning crescent represents the Crone.

The Mother image became associated with the moon, in part, because of the similarities between the swelling of the moon and its subsequent decline and the changes in a woman's body due to pregnancy. The Mother image is perhaps the most powerful and certainly the most enduring of all goddess types. She is the totality of all that is feminine. The Mother is the vessel through which all things enter into the world. She governs the fertility of animals, humans, and all life exiting in the world. One of her oldest titles is the Lady of the Beasts, for her earliest images include the Goddess with a variety of animals.

Just as the Goddess was believed to give life, she also received it back into herself. This has led some to divide the Goddess image into two polarities: the Great Mother who wields power over life and birth, and the Terrible Mother brandishing power over death and destruction. From this arose the imagery of the life-generating womb of the earth and the opposite symbol of the devouring mouth of the Underworld. It is from this connection that the Mother Goddess took on the aspects of the power of light and darkness.

The aspect of Crone sits opposite the Mother image, for physical fertility has passed from her vessel. The Crone symbolizes the accumulation of wisdom and the role of counselor. In many traditions the Crone figure is also the gatekeeper to the Underworld who escorts the dead into the Otherworld.

The aspect of Maiden within the Goddess forms represents her youthful and independent nature. Where the Mother is bound to family and the Crone to community, the Maiden is free to explore the outside world and find her own expression. She is sometimes depicted in art as a young huntress carrying a bow. The bow reflects her connection to the moon (in crescent form) and her pursuit reveals the driving force of her personal adventure.

The God

The God-form in Witchcraft is associated in symbolism with the sun and the seasons of the year. Light, fertility, death, and rebirth are all themes related to the God. Some of the oldest images of a god appear in ancient art as a male figure wearing the horns of a stag or some other horned animal.

For the early hunter societies, horned animals such as the deer provided food, clothing, and tools made from the horns. The stag became a symbol of the Great Provider, an early concept of a father-god image. Among the early hunter groups there arose a concept known as the sacred covenant between the hunter and the hunted.

The covenant consisted of an "agreement" imagined between human and animal in which the slain animal was assured of new life in exchange for his body. To accomplish this the hunters wore the horns of the animal (whether as jewelry or headgear). Through this primitive notion of a magical connection, the stag was animated and lived once again.

Through his connection with the stag, the God was known as the Lord of the Woods. He has been called by various names in many regions of Europe. To some he is Cernunnos, Herne, Dianus, Silvanus, Hu Gadarn, Dionysos, Puck, and Bacchus among others. As a horned god he represents the impregnating principle of fertility, virility, raw vitality, strength, and protection.

As humans began to settle into an agrarian society the image of the God evolved in accord with the needs of the people. The stag-horned god of the forest dwellers became the bull-horned god of the pastoral herders, and later the goat-horned god of the farmers. As people became more dependent upon agriculture, the Lord of the Woods was transformed into the Lord of the Harvest. By this era he was called such names as Green George, Jack-in-the-Green, Haxey Hood, and John Barleycorn.

The God is sometimes referred to as the Slain God, the self-sacrificing God who dies for the welfare of his people. The role of the God as the Great Provider is a role that calls for his life to be taken, whether hunted as deer or harvested as grain. The concept of the Slain God depicts the vital essence of the deity dwelling within a material vessel, which is placed within the soil to renew the fertility of the land. This was either the blood of the horned god or the seed of the god who was hooded-in-the-green (the Harvest Lord). With the establishment of the agricultural society, plant sacrifice replaced the animal sacrifice of the hunter-gatherer society.

The importance of the warmth and light of the sun to an agricultural society is significant. This is why the solstice and equinox periods were of great importance. The moon had long been associated with the Goddess figure, and the sun became the God and a consort. Solar myths became linked to the God and as a composite figure in Witchcraft he appeared as a horned deity (usually stag-horned) who was not only the Lord of the Woods, but also a solar hero identified with the Harvest Lord character.

In ancient times people believed that the sun was reborn on the day of the Winter Solstice. To acknowledge his eternal life, the evergreen tree became one of his potent symbols during the winter season. Wreaths symbolized the ever-repeating cycle of his birth, death, and resurrection. Offerings were placed and torches were lighted to encourage the return of his light and warmth.

Because the God image in Witchcraft has evolved over the centuries, absorbing various elements of folklore and folk-magic beliefs, he exhibits many characteristics. An important aspect of the God is his connection to the Underworld. To our ancient ancestors it appeared that the sun rose each day from beneath the earth. It returned there at the end of each day as well. Therefore it was believed that the sun was at home in the Underworld.

The Underworld connection to the God completes his imagery and establishes him as the Lord of the Dead. As the Sun God he is the Lord of the Living, and as the Harvest Lord he is the Slain God who renews life through his own death.

The Child of Promise

The Child of Promise in his most popular form is the reborn sun god who will reign in the coming year. He dies in the harvest season and is born again on the morning of the Winter Solstice. The God reaches adolescence in the Spring and obtains manhood by the morning of May 1. By Summer he is the formal consort of the Goddess.

The principle of the Child of Promise is not limited to the mythical theology of Witchcraft, and is found in different forms within both ritual and magic. On one level the Child of Promise is the assurance of the coming year and the renewal associated with new beginnings. On another level the Child of Promise is the manifestation of one's wishes and desires, but at the core essence lies the ancient spirit of the plant kingdom.

Tree worship appears to be among the earliest "formal" religious acts performed by humans. Elements of tree worship include the Greenman figure, spirits known as dryads, and various deities connected to the oak and other sacred trees. Eventually the spirits and deities of the forests and woodlands of our hunter-gatherer ancestors were venerated in the seasonal crops of the agrarian society.

In northern Europe, figures known as the Holly King and the Oak King arose as personifications of the forces of Nature and the spirits of the Plant Kingdom. The Oak King represents the waxing forces of Nature, and his reign begins on the Winter Solstice. This is accomplished by defeating his brother, the Holly King, in ritual combat. The Holly King symbolizes the waning forces of Nature. On the Summer Solstice the Holly King defeats the Oak King and reigns until the Winter Solstice.

The evergreen plants associated with the Yule season are symbols of the Child of Promise, who is the future Green Man and Sun God. The Yule wreath symbolizes the unbroken Wheel of the Year, the promise of life's endless cycle. The holly bough and its red berries speak of the vitality and tenacity of life. Mistletoe, as a symbol of freedom and liberation, announces the end of the waning darkness and the return of the waxing powers of light. The pine cone, as the seed bearer, perhaps best symbolizes the Child of Promise in its potential form.

The Greenman

One of the images of the God as Lord of the Plant Kingdom is the figure known as the Greenman. He is the spirit of growth and renewal, the intelligence dwelling within the meadows, fields, and forests. The earliest representation of the classic Greenman image appears in the fifth century B.C.E. in an artifact called the St. Goar pillar. The carved stone image is a blend of Etruscan art with the Celtic style of the Le Tene culture.

In Witchcraft the Greenman is associated with the ancient agricultural mystery teachings that incorporate metaphors to convey occult teachings. In the mystery teachings the Greenman is associated with the essence of intoxication, which is both physical and spiritual. The most common substance used in the mystery tradition was wine or beer, which are beverages made from grapes or grains. There was also known to be some use of hallucinogenic plants such as mushrooms and ergot mold (not uncommonly found on grain).

Ancient people believed that the spirit of the plant caused the feeling of intoxication. Once consumed, the entity released its power, which was the transforming essence of the spirit that resided in the plant. To consume the nature of the plant spirit (Greenman/Harvest Lord) was to become one with his spirit. This is the basis of the Rite of Communion found in many religions (old and new).

The earliest god forms of the agricultural mysteries are associated with the rising and dying of vegetation, which reflects the teachings of transformation. The occult tenets connected with reincarnation and transmigration are found in the cycles of life of the Plant Kingdom. The seasons of the earth (marked by the Wheel of the Year) are amplifiers and signalers of the mystical powers of the Greenman at work in the fields and forests. The goal of the agricultural mystery teachings was to link the individual to the mythos of the dying and returning god (the Harvest Lord). This connection assured one of "salvation" from the forces of death and annihilation.

The mythos of the Harvest Lord is found in the story of the passion of the flax and the dying god. The theme is set in the planting of the seed and its struggle to sprout from the earth. This is followed by its endurance of the elements as it grows to fullness. In its prime it is pulled out of the ground and subjected to thrashing, soaking, and roasting. Eventually it is combed with hackle-combs and thorns, spun into thread, and woven into linen. Finally it is cut and pierced with needles, then sown into cloth. Here then is the essence of the sacrifice of the Harvest Lord for the welfare of his people.

The Elemental Spirits

In Witchcraft there is a belief in certain spirits that assist Nature in the process of renewing and maintaining the Earth. Witches personify these forces by labeling them as the spirits assigned with elemental properties. The creative powers of the elemental spirits are evoked by Witches to empower the gathering circles used for ritual and magical purpose.

One of the earliest references to Witches working with elemental spirits appears in the *Compendium Maleficarum,* published in 1608. The *Compendium* was written by an Ambrosian monk named Francesco Guazzo. Here Guazzo wrote that Witches "have dealings" with spirits of Fire, Air, Earth, and Water.[1]

In a long-standing occult tradition the elemental spirits are known as Gnomes, Sylphs, Salamanders, and Undines. According to these teachings the four primary elements of Earth, Air, Fire, and Water consist of both a vaporous spirit form and a tangible material substance. Each of these exists in separate dimensions, which some people refer to as the Physical World and the Supernatural World.

Within the Supernatural World the elemental beings occupy their own elemental regions. Occult teachings assign Gnomes to Earth, Sylphs to Air, Salamanders to Fire, and Undines to Water. Elemental beings are considered to be creatures of a single nature related entirely to the property of their corresponding element. Just as fish are creatures of the Water and birds are creatures of the Air, each elemental is unique in form and function in a way that is appropriate to its elemental environment.

Gnomes inhabit the elemental material of the Earth's spiritual dimension, which is the metaphysical counterpart of the material substance. Their actions affect the presence and quality of mineral deposits, the erosion of rock, and the formation of crystals and other geological formations. Gnomes often appear to humans as dwarfs.

Sylphs inhabit the elemental substance of the atmosphere, which is the spiritual medium of the air that surrounds our planet. Their activity affects the gathering of clouds, the formation of snowflakes, and the growth and maturity of all plant life. Sylphs often appear to humans as fairies.

Salamanders inhabit the elemental substance of Fire. The activity of Salamanders has a profound effect on the process of creating and maintaining temperature. It is through their activity that fire exists and can be used by humankind. Salamanders often appear to humans in the shape of small lizards that dart about quickly.

Undines inhabit the elemental substance of the Earth's Waters, whether in liquid or vaporous form. The activity of Undines causes the formation of water and its coalescence. The presence of Undines purifies water and helps keep it supportive of life. Undines often appear to humans as mermaids.

The Watchers

In Witchcraft there is a belief in a spiritual race of beings known as the Watchers. The Watchers guard and protect the portals to and from the Otherworld, which reside at the four cardinal points of north, east, south, and west. At each of the four points stands what Witches call a Watchtower, which serves as the place where the Watchers gather when ritual gathering circles are cast.

Although the Watchers now appear to be viewed as a highly evolved race that dwells in the spiritual dimension, their origins in lore and legend are rooted in primitive belief systems. Over the centuries they have evolved from simple guardians of allocated land to angel-like beings and keepers of dimensional doorways.

The first clear traces of the Watchers appear in archaic Roman religion, which was derived from Etruscan beliefs. In the early days of Rome it was little more than a small farming community located within the Etruscan Empire. Plots of land were allocated in squares and a spirit known as a Lare protected each plot. Small towers were built at the crossroads, and an altar was set before them upon which offerings were given.

In archaic Roman religion the guardian Lare spirits were associated with these towers and with demarcation in general, as well as seasonal themes related to agriculture. Over the course of time the Lare spirit was moved from the fields and venerated in the house where it became an ancestral spirit, and a protector of hearth and home.

The term "Watchers" was also used in the early stellar cults of Mesopotamia. In this system four *royal* stars (known as Lords) appeared that were referred to as the Watchers. Each one of these stars ruled over one of the four cardinal points common to astrology. The Star Aldebaran (when it marked the Vernal Equinox) held the position of Watcher of the East. Regulus (marking the Summer Solstice) was Watcher of the South. Antares (marking the Autumn Equinox) was Watcher of the West. Fomalhaut (marking the Winter Solstice) was Watcher of the North.

In the star myths the Watchers themselves were depicted as gods who guarded the Heavens and the Earth. The nature of the Watchers (as well as their status) was altered by the successive lunar and solar cults that replaced the older stellar cults. Eventually the Greeks reduced the Watchers to the gods of the four winds and named them Boreas, Eurus, Notus, and Zephyrus.

Christian theologians, in their attempts to discredit pagan beliefs, assigned the Watchers to an evil class of fallen angels known as the "principalities of the air." Earlier mystical Hebrew sects organized the Watchers into an archangel hierarchy. According to this system, the Watchers were ruled over by four great Watchers known as Michael, Gabriel, Raphael, and Auriel.

In the Old Testament (Daniel 4:13–17) there is reference made to the Irin/Watchers, which appear to be an order of angels. In early Hebrew lore the Irin were a high order of angels that sat on the supreme Judgment Council of the Heavenly Court. In the Apocryphal Books of Enoch and Jubilees, the Watchers were sent to Earth to teach law and justice to humankind. It is these same angels who are referred to as the "Sons of God" in the Book of Genesis.

Richard Cavendish, in his book *The Powers of Evil*, suggests that the giants mentioned in Genesis 6:4 may be primal gods known as the Titans of Greek Mythology, which he implies share a relationship to the Watchers. Cavendish notes an ancient belief that the stars were the "eyes of night" and theorizes that the title "The Watchers" is derived from this ancient concept.[2]

While the foreign concepts we have examined here are interesting, they were absent from European thought until the influence of Middle Eastern concepts arrived when formal trade was established between the two regions. In ancient Europe the term "Watchtower" had two meanings. The first meaning referred to a physical structure, typically attached to a castle or any fortification. The second meaning referred to a military fighting unit that defended towns and villages while the army was away engaged in war (similar to the function of the modern National Guard).

The Elven and Fairy Race

According to ancient lore, Elves are an ancient race that predate the appearance of humans on the earth. In myth and legend, elves have superior intelligence, and are highly skilled in the magical arts. They also possess secret knowledge of the healing arts and have heightened physical and psychic senses.

There appears to be a universal and timeless belief in the existence of beings that are not gods or spirits, and who are similar in many ways to humans. Although sharing a likeness of form with humans, these beings display powers and attributes that are quite different from those of humankind. Such beings have been referred to as the Elven Race for many centuries. For a more in-depth investigation of the Fairy race, my book, *The Wiccan Mysteries*, contains material related to these mysterious beings.[3]

Folklorists use the term Elven to designate fairies, gnomes, sprites, leprechauns, pixies, knockers, nymphs, and other such beings. All of these so-called supernatural beings are then placed in three categories: Light elves, Dark elves, and Dusk elves. Light elves have the ability to shapeshift and cross at will between the dimensions of time and space. Dark elves are associated with underground places such as burrows, mounds, caves, and so forth. Dusk elves are those beings tied to Nature through trees, meadows, fields, hedgerows, mountains, lakes, and streams.

Some folklorists point to an interesting connection between the old tales of human encounters with fairies and contemporary encounters with aliens from other worlds. In both cases there are reports of mysterious lights, small human-like creatures with odd features (and often with green skin), physical abduction, and loss of time and memory. Some social anthropologists suggest that this "phenomena" has been around since the beginning, and that each generation creates a mythos to explain it. Therefore, to the medieval mind these creatures were fairies, and to the modern mind they are extraterrestrial beings. If such creatures exist, then what are they? There is no common unified agreement among Witches.

Our agrarian ancestors believed that fairies dwelled beneath mounds in the earth. Since seeds went into the ground and plants sprang forth from beneath the soil, a belief arose that the hidden race of beings controlled the fertility of the land.

Some kings, such as King Olaf (circa 1031 C.E.), were believed to have elven bloodlines. In the King Arthur mythos, the welfare of the king is tied to the welfare of the land. Here we see an interesting connection between fertility, kingship, and the Elven race.

The importance of the land and assurance of the fertility of the Plant Kingdom is at the core of fairy and human relationships. This is demonstrated in the seasons believed to have been sacred to the Fairy race and the seasonal rites observed by modern Witches. These seasons match those of the Wheel of the Year, also known as the Witches' Sabbats.

Let us turn now to the next chapter and examine the rituals of Witchcraft and how they apply not only to the seasons of the year, but also to the mystical seasons of the soul.

ELEVEN

Rituals

The rituals of Witchcraft are based primarily upon a veneration of Nature and an acknowledgment that humankind is intimately linked to the cycles of Nature. A formal ritual allows the Witch to directly participate in the dance of Nature at any given season. This is why the rituals of Witchcraft mark the solstice and equinox periods of the Earth and the seasonal periods that lie directly between each one. Collectively this is called the Wheel of the Year, and is envisioned as an eight-spoke wagon wheel.

The Wheel of the Year also reflects the spiritual teachings of Witchcraft. These are mirrored in the metaphors contained within the basic format of the mythical images expressed in any given ritual. The myths around which the structure of a ritual is formed speak to the mystical energy that permeates the rites of Witchcraft. They are stories that express deeper truths.

On a mundane level the rituals that comprise the Wheel of the Year are rooted in the fire festival rites of pre-Christian European religion. The seasons of the year when these bonfires were typically lighted were Spring, Summer, Autumn, and Winter. At the cross-quarters in February, May, August Eve, and October other bonfires burned as well.

In ancient times it was the custom to drive the flocks and cattle through the bonfire's smoke, and by some accounts over the ebbing flames or coals. Torches were lighted from the bonfires and carried through the planting fields, orchards, and pastures. Ashes from the bonfire were scattered over the ground in a belief that this would make the soil of the coming season fertile again. According to oral tradition hot embers were carried back to the hearths in a race. It was believed that great luck for the entire year would come to whoever first entered his or her house with the sacred embers of the bonfire.

Our ancestors believed that their participation was needed in order for the seasons to change, and to keep the sun's warmth from escaping eventual return. This was due, in part, to the belief that humans are not separate and isolated from Nature. For our ancestors, Nature was not a resource to take from, but was instead a partner in mutual survival. This partnership required cooperation and teamwork. It is still an important philosophy, but regretfully one not shared today by many humans who have financial and political power over matters that affect the health of the environment in which we must all live.

For Witches the "turning of the Wheel" is still an important aspect of practicing religion and spirituality. On one level it is simply an acknowledgment of the cycles of Nature (a process that significantly affects all our lives) as well as an opportunity to align oneself with the specific pattern of energy present at any given season. Such an alliance establishes the Witch in harmony with the prevailing forces instead of being pitted against them. It is a practical and healthy way to live each season that is given to us.

On another level, participation in the turning of the Wheel connects the Witch with the divine emanations that lie behind the cycles of Nature. Humans have long sensed something deeper at work within Nature, and have attempted to personify it as spirits or deities. Myths and legends then formed around these personifications in an attempt to explain the origins and actions of this mystical "something." In other words, myths were tales about how it all worked and interacted with itself. Each aspect, or part of the process, was given an identity in the form of a particular being within Nature.

Ancient myths still speak to the human spirit and continue to be told over countless centuries. In the popular movie *Lord of the Rings*, it is recounted that history became myth, and myth became legend. In a sense myths are historical in the respect that they represent the thinking of the times, the things that were important to the storyteller. Myths are not sheer fantasy, but are captured "snapshots" of the evolution of religious and spiritual thought (even though this may be clouded by the folklore environment surrounding them). Therefore myths contain cultural truths transformed into imagery that is expressed through the presentation of simple stories.

It is readily apparent that the myths and legends of various cultures all reflect the commonality of human conception, experience, and expression. As mythologist Joseph Campbell pointed out, the role of the hero in myth and legend is universal. So too, it seems, is the need to identify ourselves with the hero figure. Through identification an individual feels linked with the hero and experiences (as well as accomplishes) what the hero does.[1]

The hero figure faces fear and vanquishes it. Heroes meet challenges and successfully master them despite any and all obstacles. The hero leads the way into the labyrinth and does not become lost. Even when a hero meets death, the hero is either transformed or resurrected, but is never ultimately conquered. Through identification with the hero figure an individual joins his or her fate to that of the hero. This is, in essence, the key to embracing the image and concept of the Slain God in Witchcraft. To embrace a deity that dies and is reborn assures the follower of rebirth through his or her association with the divine agent or intermediary. We see the same principle in Christianity where its followers believe that their salvation is linked to the death and resurrection of the figure known as Jesus Christ.

Concerning a Mythos

When examining the rituals of Witchcraft two basic patterns readily appear. One system depicts a story that involves a named God and Goddess figure. Each Sabbat of the year features their relationship to one another and to Nature. The story is one of continuity in which any other deities or spirits that appear share an integrated relationship with one another, and a congruent cultural link that demonstrates their mutual origins and evolution.

In such a system the names of the God and Goddess remain consistent with their myths as expressed in each season. When other deities or spirits appear they are traceable to one another as well as to the primary deities, and all share a general mythical and cultural connection. The names of the Sabbats in such a system conform to a common cultural etymology demonstrating their colloquial nature. We'll refer to this system as "Theme A."

The other system, which we will label "Theme B," resembles a patchwork quilt depicting deities and spirits that share no culturally integrated myth or legend (although they often appear in the same culture, but have separate themes and no direct links). In this sense such characters appear isolated from one another, and their appearance in the Wheel of the Year reflects a confined seasonal expression that lacks solidarity with the other characters. One example is the birth of a sun god at the Winter Solstice who is not the same god that dies as the Harvest Lord in Autumn. Another example is the appearance of seasonal characters that share no mythical or allegorical relationship with the primary God and Goddess of the system. In Theme B, the names of the Sabbats typically are those of mixed cultures and share no former relationship as integrated elements of a preexisting whole.

For people just beginning to explore the Craft, Theme B systems can be confusing and appear more complex than they actually are. By contrast, Theme A can appear too structured, which can deter some "free-spirited" people from exploring this type of system. In the final analysis, it is wise to explore both so as to gain a greater vision for one's personal walk. There is no such thing as useless knowledge or experience.

For the purposes of introducing a mythos in this book, I have chosen to present a theme of continuity. Alongside this I will also present the popular variations that the reader should become familiar with when encountering Witchcraft Traditions. The more information you collect, the better you will be prepared to make the choices that will be correct for you as a unique individual.

Wheel of the Year Mythos

In Witchcraft the general Wheel of the Year contains a mythos based upon the courtship of the God and Goddess, and the son they bear. In a metaphorical sense the mythos also reflects the journey of the soul through material life, for in the tale each of us is the God and Goddess, as well as the reborn sun, the shapeshifting moon, and the Harvest Lord. Through identification with these mythical characters we come to know the various aspects of our own being. Through participation in the Wheel of the Year we come into direct contact with the spiritual forces that empower and direct our lives.

The mythos begins in the season that many Witches call Samhain, for this is the Witches' New Year celebration. At this time the God and Goddess dwell in the Underworld, the realm of procreation. The Underworld is the dark womb from which all life issues forth and to which all life returns. In the Underworld the God and Goddess meet as the polarities of Divine Spirit, and come to love one another. This speaks to us of our own male and female polarities within, and of the need for integration and personal balance. When we are alone in the darkness we need only embrace that which separates us from life, and we shall be reborn into the light of day.

In Witchcraft the Winter Solstice marks the rebirth of the sun, conceived in the Underworld through the union of the God and Goddess (although in some traditions the mating takes place at the Spring and/or Fall Equinox). On the day of the Winter Solstice the sun appears as a mythical infant called the Child of Promise. By late December the world has grown cold and seemingly lifeless (especially in regions where snow falls).

The Child of Promise is a sign of the covenant between all living things and the God and Goddess. The covenant assures the return of warmth, light, and life in an endless cycle of the year. In this we see the eternal life of our own soul, reborn in many cycles of life on this world and others to come. Underlying this is the guiding light of the divine spark within, which assures us that deity walks always by our side.

At the beginning of February a celebration is held that many Witches call Imbolc. In the general mythos this is the time when the sun god reaches adolescence. It is also the time of purification as Winter moves closer to Spring, and preparations begin for the coming season of growth. In Celtic traditions this is the holy day of the goddess Brigid, a deity associated with fire, healing, and fertility. At this season we realize the need to purify ourselves of the negativity and self-imposed limitations that restricted our growth and evolution as spiritual beings during the past year. We heal ourselves and work toward making our lives fertile for abundance in the coming season.

In the Witches' mythos the Spring Equinox marks the return of the Goddess from the Underworld. With her return to the world of the living, the life force of Nature is once again restored. Soon with the warmth of the sun upon the soil, the life within the seed will awaken. The cycle of regeneration begins anew, and from what appeared to be death comes new life. Here we find the teaching that life is not extinguished by death, but that death brings new life. This strengthens the role of reincarnation in the beliefs of Witchcraft, and reminds us that the death of the flesh is only a transition. Transition at this time reminds us that we must prepare the soil of our lives and plant the seeds of our desire for the coming harvest that we wish to reap.

On the first day of May a festival occurs that is known by many Witches as Beltane. In the mythos this is the courtship period between the God and Goddess. Beltane contains perhaps the strongest fertility symbolism of all of the Witches' Sabbats. Many ancient fertility themes have survived in the rites of May, such as the Maypole, which once symbolized the potent and powerful force that impregnates Nature and brings forth fruit and grain in the Summer. Here we see ourselves in our full potentiality, wherein we are both the seed and the power to awaken the seed.

The Summer Solstice marks the period of growth to fullness, the ripe harvest to come. The signs (both literally and figuratively) of the fruits of our labor are present in this season. In the Wheel of the Year mythos, the God and Goddess are wed together at this time. The world reflects the abundance that arises from the union of the male and female polarities. In many Celtic systems a set of characters appear known as the Oak King and Holly King. Here they represent the waxing and waning forces of Nature in opposition to one another, for the brothers fight one another in a contest for seasonal reign.

In many Aegean/Mediterranean systems, the waning and waxing forces of Nature are depicted as the Stag and the Wolf.

Here the waxing and waning forces of Nature are portrayed in the natural order that maintains balance. At the time of the Summer Solstice we evaluate the state of our lives and acknowledge our participation or lack therein, which addresses the core issue of responsibility. Are we living life according to balance, and if not, then what forces have we allowed to direct things?

The Harvest Season marks the next ritual celebration in Witchcraft. In many Celtic systems this ritual occasion is called Lughnasadh, reportedly named after the Celtic solar deity Lugh. In the mythos of Witchcraft, this is the season in which the God is slain in the reaping of the harvest. He is slain at the height of his power, and his life essence is given back to the soil. Thus the return of the vital essence assures the fertility of the soil and therefore the growth and harvest in the following year. Here we acknowledge the attainment of what our energies were directed upon, which in accord will be a bountiful or meager harvest.

The next festival season in Witchcraft is marked by the Autumn Equinox. In the mythos this is the time at which the Goddess descends into the Underworld in search of her lover who was slain in the harvest. The life force of Nature now retreats from the world to sleep beneath the soil. Here we begin to examine what must die in our own lives in order for rejuvenation and renewal to take place. What habits and practices are beneficial and productive? Which ones are destructive or nonproductive? During this season we seek discernment and the wisdom to know what needs to be released from our lives. This leads us back to the season of October and the procreative darkness in which we will plant the seeds of the coming harvest of our lives (our own Child of Promise). We have now turned the Wheel of the Year one complete cycle.

Ritual Names

The names used in Witchcraft for each Sabbat differ according to cultural expression or eclectic taste. In the early twentieth century many popular systems of Witchcraft used the Christianized names of the old Pagan festivals. These names came from the late Middle Ages period (see chart on p. 178, column 2).

Following the exposure of the Craft to the public, circa 1954, many Traditions used a name system more in keeping with the original Pagan theme (column 3). In the early 1970s another set of names arose as eclectic systems became highly popular (column 4). In Italian Witchcraft (one of the oldest systems to survive into modern times) a different set of names are used. The names are shown in English in column 5 of the chart.

The Rituals

There are many books currently available that contain formal rituals for both group and solitary practice. Therefore my goal is not to provide you with more of the same, but instead to present the symbolism that focuses on each of the seasons, and the essential reasons for performing each ritual. I encourage you to expand and customize this material to fit your needs, both now and in the future. See appendix three for suggested reading.

Ritual is a means of achieving a state of consciousness in which an individual can interface with the inner mechanisms. Ritual draws the individual into full and complete participation on all levels: mind, body, and spirit. It is very important to be in the moment when performing a ritual. Select a time and a place in which you will not be disturbed or interrupted.

Before beginning any ritual, take a few moments to sit quietly (breathing deeply and slowly) and let go of the mundane world around you. Turn out all artificial lights, using only the flames of a candle or oil lamp. When you are ready to begin, handle each ritual item with deliberate reverence, and think

Sabbat Names — Origin/History

Date*	Middle Ages (old Pagan)	Original Pagan (circa 1954)	Eclectic (1970s)	Italian
Oct. 31	Hallowmas	Samhain	Samhain	Shadowfest
Dec. 21	Yule	Yule	Yule	Winter Solstice
Feb. 2	Candlemas	Imbolc	Imbolc	Lupercus
Mar. 21	Lady Day	Spring Equinox	Ostara	Spring Equinox
May 1	Roodmas	Beltane	Beltane	Goddess Day
June 21	St. John's Day	Midsummer	Litha	Summer Solstice
Aug. 1	Lammas	Lughnasadh	Lughnasadh	Cornucopia
Sept. 21	Michaelmas	Autumn Equinox	Mabon	Autumn Equinox

* Dates may vary slightly from one system to another.

about its symbolism. Emotionally invest yourself in the ritual and never perform any act or recite any words in a lackadaisical manner.

If you are a beginner, the following rituals do not require the formal casting of a circle. However you will need to sprinkle a circle of salt large enough to sit in with your altar. This will be your setting of sacred space. A small table or stand can serve as your personal altar. Read over each ritual completely before attempting to perform any rite. This will not only familiarize you with the procedure, but will also inform you of the items you will need during the ritual itself. Many of the ritual items, such as wreaths, brooms, and corn dolls, can be obtained in miniature form at most hobby and craft stores.

On a final note, the following rituals are not representative of any one specific tradition of Witchcraft. Instead they have been designed as a basic framework structure that demonstrates the core essence of the seasons as they relate to our needs. I encourage the reader at some later point to explore the rituals of specific traditions. This will greatly enhance your understanding of the Wheel of the Year.

Samhain

The key alignments of this season are Otherworld connection and creative potential. Both are related to the darkness of night (not the darkness of spirit). Therefore, you will want to use a symbol that connects to both concepts. The traditional objects are the skull and the cauldron. The skull represents the spirits in the Otherworld (literally one's ancestors). It can be made of anything, with the exception of plastic. The cauldron represents the womb of generative life. It can be made of metal (preferred) or of heat-resistant ceramic material.

On your altar place two black candles at the opposite end from where you will be positioned. The candles should be several inches apart, and from your perspective will be to your left and right. These candles serve as the sides of the doorway in the Otherworld. In the center of your altar place the skull and secure a red candle on its top. This will represent the living connection between you and the spirits on the other side. Red symbolizes the life force of blood.

In front of the skull place a small cauldron. Ideally the skull should be larger than the cauldron so that the skull is visible during the rite. Close at hand to your right, place a ritual bell. The final item needed is a small plate and a cup. On the plate you will want to place some food offerings (fruit, cheese, and beans are preferred). In the cup pour some water, wine, or mead. This is often referred to as the meal of the dead, an offering to appease the spirits of the Otherworld. Place these items on your altar to the left side. This should leave some work space directly in front of you on the altar.

When you are ready to begin, light the black candles from left to right. Ring the altar bell three times and then recite the following:

> I call to the Goddess and the God to bless this ritual, and to protect all against harm on this sacred night. I call upon my guides and guardians to gather around me and to protect me from all misdeeds.

Next, ring the bell three times, light the red candle, and say:

> In the names of the God and Goddess, I call to the spirits beyond the veil between this world and the next. Come and partake of the offerings I freely give here upon this altar. Enter in peace and leave in peace.

At this stage, take a piece of parchment and write a request. This should be something positive that you would like to have happen in the coming twelve months. The first time you perform this rite, keep the request simple and realistic. As a guide to some possible requests, please note: Do not ask for money, ask for prosperity. Do not ask for someone specific to fall in love with you, ask that someone compatible be drawn into your life. Do not ask for revenge or harm upon another, ask to be freed from the influence or power of your enemies. The "powers that be" see further and with much greater wisdom than we do. Give the Universe some room to work in, and understand that the future outcome requires your full participation in achieving your goals. In the Craft there are no free rides and you have no servants. Instead you have faithful companions and powerful allies.

Once your request is written on the parchment, speak your wish out loud: "In the names of the God and Goddess, I request _____." Then fold the parchment three times and place it in the cauldron. Next, light a match, set the parchment on fire, and say:

> By the transforming power of fire, may these words become the manifestation of my desire. Spirits of the Otherworld, aid me from beyond. God and Goddess, bless my request and protect all from harm in the fulfillment of my desire.

When the parchment is consumed, gently blow the smoke with your breath directly toward the red candle. Following this, increase the force of your next exhalations until the red candle is blown out. Then ring the bell three times and say, "Spirits, depart now in peace, and return to your realm." Next, gently blow the smoke from the red candle out between the two black candles. Continue until there is no longer any smoke rising from either the cauldron or the red candle.

The final phase of the ritual turns now to giving offerings to the God and Goddess. This can be something as simple as putting flowers in a special vase, to singing or playing a musical instrument in their honor. Before making an offering, say:

God and Goddess, I thank you for your presence in
my life, and for walking with me along my path.
Please accept this offering as a token of my love.

Once the offering phase is completed you can remove the
altar items, clean them, and put them away. Take all of the ashes
from the cauldron, and somewhere outside in a private place,
face the east (or if wind is present, turn your back to it) and blow
the ashes into the air. Imagine that the wind is carrying your desire off to be made manifest.

Yule

The key alignments of this season are rebirth and renewal. Both
are related to the light of the sun. Therefore you will want to
use a symbol that connects to both concepts. The traditional objects are the evergreen wreath and the yule log. The wreath represents the repeating cycle of life, as well as the promise of
survival, which is symbolized by the evergreen tree. The Yule
log, traditionally pine or oak, represents the sun and the sun
god. This is a symbolic remnant of tree worship from ancient
times when people believed that the gods dwelled in trees.

On your altar place two green candles at the opposite end
from where you will be positioned. The candles should be several inches apart, and from your perspective will be to your left
and right. These candles serve as the symbols of life in the material world and the spiritual world. Secure three red candles to
the Yule log, symbolizing the vitality of the Evergreen God. In
the center of your altar place the wreath with a yellow candle in
the middle opening. This will represent the living connection between the sun and the promise of renewal and rebirth.

In front of the wreath place a small cauldron with an orange
votive candle inside. The altar can be decorated with other traditional symbols such as holly and mistletoe. Leave room for a ritual bell, which is placed on the right side of the altar. The final

item needed is a small plate and a cup for offerings. Nuts, sweets, and wine or mead is traditional.

When you are ready to begin, light the green candles from left to right. Ring the altar bell three times, and then recite the following:

> I call to the Goddess and the God to bless this ritual
> on this sacred day of rebirth.

Next, ring the bell three times, light the yellow candle, and say:

> In the names of the God and Goddess, I call to the spirit of the sun who is reborn this day. Come, partake of the offerings I freely give here upon this altar, and remember your promise to return life in fullness. And through this my life, too, shall be renewed.

At this stage, take the yellow candle and use it to light the votive candle in the cauldron. Then recite:

> The fire of the Year God is passed into the Child of Promise. The Child of Light is born, the Child of Promise has come. In a new light shall I walk in the days to come.

The final phase of the ritual turns now to giving offerings to the God and Goddess. Before presenting the offerings, say:

> God and Goddess, I thank you for your presence in my life, and for awakening the new light of the coming seasons. Please accept this offering as a token of my love.

Place your hands, palms up, one on each side of the offering plate as a welcome. Once the offering phase is completed you can remove the altar items (except for the votive candle), clean them, and put them away. Allow the votive candle to burn out by itself. Afterward clean the cauldron and put it away.

Imbolc

The key alignments of this season are purity and growth. Both are related to the light of the sun. The traditional objects of this season are the candle wheel and the strawman doll. The candle wheel represents the growing cycle of life, the waxing light of the sun. You can use a hoop or a wreath to serve as the wheel and secure the candles to it. The strawman doll represents the young sun god. This is a symbolic remnant of the Harvest Lord/ Greenman image, which our ancestors believed lived in the trees and plants.

On your altar place two white candles at the opposite end from where you will be positioned. The candles should be several inches apart, and from your perspective will be to your left and right. These candles serve as the symbols of purification in the material world and the spiritual world. In the center of your altar place the sun wheel with twelve white candles (birthday size). This will represent the living connection between the sun and waxing cycle of Nature. In front of the sun wheel place the strawman doll.

The altar can be decorated with other traditional symbols such as pine cones and acorns. Leave room for a ritual bell, which is placed on the right side of the altar. The final item needed is a small plate for offerings of pumpkin seeds, nuts, and bread. A cup of milk is also traditional.

When you are ready to begin, light the white altar candles from left to right. Ring the altar bell three times, and then recite the following:

> I call to the Goddess and the God to bless this ritual
> on this sacred day of purification and growth.

Next, ring the bell three times, light the sun wheel candles, and say:

> In the names of the God and Goddess, I call to the
> waxing spirit of the sun. Come, partake of the offer-

ings I freely give here upon this altar. Grow in strength and purity. And through this my life, too, is purified, and I am assured of growth in the coming seasons.

Raise the strawman doll up and pass it over the sun wheel in a full circle (moving clockwise). Then return him in front of the sun wheel. The final phase of the ritual turns now to giving offerings to the God and Goddess. Before presenting the offerings, say:

God and Goddess, I thank you for your presence in my life, and for purifying the light within and without. May your blessings of growth and increase permeate the coming seasons. Please accept this offering as a token of my love.

Place your hands, palms up, one on each side of the offering plate as a welcome. Once the offering phase is completed you can remove the altar items (except for the sun wheel and strawman doll), clean them, and put them away. Allow the sun wheel candles to burn out. When the candles have burned away, hang the strawman doll in a window that faces east. Remove him and put him away after his first meeting with the sunrise. Later when you plant your garden, you can dip the strawman doll in water and anoint the seeds by shaking the wet doll over them.

Spring Equinox

The key alignments of this season are regeneration and renewal. Both are related to the feminine principle in Nature. The traditional symbolic objects of this season are the egg and the cauldron. The egg represents birth in the "breaking through" process, also reflected in the return of the Goddess from the Underworld. The cauldron is the womb of the Goddess, from which all things are born.

On your altar place two light-green candles at the opposite end from where you will be positioned. The candles should be several inches apart, and from your perspective will be to your left and right. These candles serve as the symbols of life renewed. In the center of your altar place the cauldron with the egg inside it. This will represent the vessel of life (in the Underworld) returning through the vessel of regeneration.

In front of the cauldron place a small red votive candle. The altar can be decorated with other traditional symbols such as flowers, hare images, seeds, and so forth. Leave room for a ritual bell, which is placed on the right side of the altar. The final item needed is a small plate and a cup for offerings. Bread and cake are traditional, along with either wine or mead.

When you are ready to begin, light the green candles from left to right. Ring the altar bell three times, and then recite the following:

> I call to the Goddess and the God to bless this ritual
> on this sacred day, which marks the return of life to
> the world.

Next, ring the bell three times, light the red votive candle, and say:

> In the names of the God and Goddess, I call to the
> spirit of return and regeneration. Come, partake of
> the offerings I freely give here upon this altar. As you
> awaken the sleeping seeds, awaken also the seeds of
> my own life that are the abilities I possess to accom-
> plish my goals.

At this stage, take the egg from the cauldron, hold it up, and recite:

> From the darkness beneath the earth, the life-giving
> vessel has returned. All is rebirth, all is renewal.

Set the egg on the altar where it will be safe. The final phase of the ritual turns now to giving offerings to the God and Goddess. Before presenting the offerings, say:

> God and Goddess, I thank you for your presence in
> my life, and for return of life for the coming seasons.
> Please accept this offering as a token of my love.

Place your hands, palms up, one on each side of the offering plate as a welcome. Once the offering phase is completed you can remove the altar items (except for the egg), clean them, and put them away.

Take the egg to your garden and crack it open on the ground. If you do not have a garden, then use a pot of soil. As you pour the egg out onto the soil, say:

> The land is renewed by the return of the Goddess,
> the vessel of life.

Leave the egg undisturbed for twenty-four hours, and then mix it in the soil. If you're using a pot of soil, bury the egg several inches deep and leave it untouched for three days. Afterward remove the soil, but save a handful for growing a potted plant (mix this soil with some new soil).

Beltane

The key alignments of this season are fertility and union. Both are related to the joining of the male and female polarities. The traditional tool of this season is the mortar and pestle. The mortar represents the womb and the pestle symbolizes the phallus. The importance of the mortar and pestle is that it is a unified symbol that requires both elements. Separately their intended use is lost or greatly diminished.

On your altar place a red and a green candle at the opposite end from where you will be positioned. The candles should be several inches apart, and from your perspective will be to your left (green candle) and right (red candle). These candles serve as the symbols of the male and female polarities. In the center of your altar place the mortar and pestle, side by side. Set a pink votive candle in front of the mortar and pestle.

The altar can be decorated with other traditional symbols such as flowers and colored ribbons (red and white). Leave room for a ritual bell, which is placed on the right side of the altar. The final item needed is a small bowl for an offering of porridge, custard, or pudding. A cup of May wine is also traditional (essentially a white wine, chilled, and mixed with some strawberries and a few woodruff leaves).

When you are ready to begin, light the altar candles from left to right. Ring the altar bell three times, then recite the following:

> I call to the Goddess and the God to bless this ritual
> on this sacred day of fertility and unity.

Next, ring the bell three times, light the pink candle, and say:

> In the names of the God and Goddess, I call to the essence of the feminine and masculine spirit. Come, partake of the offerings I freely give here upon this altar. Unite in creation and increase. And through this my life, too, shall become fertile and fruitful in the coming seasons.

Place the pestle in the mortar and say:

> Male to female, phallus to womb, energy to formation. Together they create and generate the gift of life.

The final phase of the ritual turns now to giving offerings to the God and Goddess. Before presenting the offerings, say:

> God and Goddess, I thank you for your presence in my life, and for the fertile and creative essence within and without. May your blessings of fertility and fruitfulness permeate the coming seasons. Please accept this offering as a token of my love.

Place your hands, palms up, one on each side of the offering plate as a welcome. Once the offering phase is completed you can remove the altar items (except for the mortar and pestle). If you have any seeds that you want to plant, place them in the mortar for blessings. You can also place an object in the mortar that is associated with something you wish to increase or see become fruitful, for example, the key to a business or an investment statement, etc.

Summer Solstice

The key alignments of this season are ripeness and rapport. The traditional objects of this season are the red rose and the leaf mask. The rose represents the Goddess in the fullness and beauty of the blossom. The leaf mask symbolizes the God in one of his primal forms, linked to the land and to the sun. The fresh leaf can be oak, holly, or ivy. Eyes, nose, and a mouth should be painted or cut out on the leaf.

On your altar place two green candles at the opposite end from where you will be positioned. The candles should be several inches apart, and from your perspective will be to your left and right. These candles serve as the symbols of ripeness and fullness. In the center of your altar place the red rose and the leaf mask, side by side. This will symbolize the union of the God and Goddess. Set a green votive candle in front of them.

The altar can be decorated with a variety of flowers, and the herbs known as vervain and St. John's Wort. Leave room for a ritual bell, which is placed on the right side of the altar. The final item needed is a small plate for offerings of fruit and vegetables. A cup of mead is also traditional.

When you are ready to begin, light the altar candles from left to right. Ring the altar bell three times, then recite the following:

> I call to the Goddess and the God to bless this ritual
> on this sacred day of ripeness and union.

Next, ring the bell three times, light the green votive candle, and say:

> In the names of the God and Goddess, I call to the spirit of rapport that unites all polarities. Come, partake of the offerings I freely give here upon this altar. Join and become greater than the whole. And through this my life, too, shall be abundant in the coming season.

The final phase of the ritual turns now to giving offerings to the God and Goddess. Before presenting the offerings, say:

> God and Goddess, I thank you for your presence in my life, and for the gift of growth and increase. May your blessings permeate the coming season. Please accept this offering as a token of my love.

Place your hands, palms up, one on each side of the offering plate as a welcome. Once the offering phase is completed you can remove the altar items (except for the rose and leaf mask), clean them, and put them away. In a private area outside set the rose on the ground and place the leaf mask over it. Leave them undisturbed and do not retrieve them later.

Lughnasadh

The key alignments of this season are harvest and abundance. The traditional objects of this season are the sheaf, the blade, and the corn doll. The sheaf represents the abundant harvest, the blade is the reaper, and the corn doll is the spirit of the field. This is symbolic of the Harvest Lord figure.

On your altar place two green candles at the opposite end from where you will be positioned. The candles should be several inches apart, and from your perspective will be to your left and right. These candles serve as the symbols of abundance and gain. In the center of your altar place the sheaf, the blade, and the corn doll next to each other. In front of this put a whole bread loaf (unsliced whole-grain wheat is good). Place a yellow candle (birthday size) in the center of the loaf.

The altar can be decorated with other traditional symbols such as seasonal berries and other fruit. Leave room for a ritual bell, which is placed on the right side of the altar. The final item needed is a small plate for offerings of oat, corn bread, or barley cakes. A cup of mead or glass of beer is also traditional.

When you are ready to begin, light the altar candles from left to right. Ring the altar bell three times, and then recite the following:

> I call to the Goddess and the God to bless this ritual
> on this sacred day of harvest and gain.

Next, ring the bell three times, light the loaf candle, and say:

> In the names of the God and Goddess, I call to the
> spirit of gathering and abundance. Come, partake of
> the offerings I freely give here upon this altar. Grant
> the fruits of all labor. And through this my life, too,
> shall be abundant and gainful in the coming seasons.

Take the knife and lay the edge on the loaf. At the same time as you cut into the bread, also blow out the candle. Remove the candle and cut the bread into three sections. Take one small piece of bread from each section, and a cup of mead or glass of wine. Set them in front of you on the altar. Then recite:

> For there are three great mysteries: Birth, Life, and
> Death.

Eat the three small portions of bread and drink some of the mead/wine. Next, recite the following:

> May I grow in knowledge and wisdom, and may the
> mysteries reveal themselves to me.

The final phase of the ritual turns now to giving offerings to the God and Goddess. Before presenting the offerings say:

> God and Goddess, I thank you for your presence in my life, and for the abundance you grant within and without. May your blessings of harvest and gain permeate the coming seasons. Please accept this offering as a token of my love.

Place your hands, palms up, one on each side of the offering plate as a welcome. Once the offering phase is completed you can remove the altar items. Pour the wine out upon the soil and toss the pieces of bread up into the air and away from you. Do not retrieve them.

Autumn Equinox

The key alignments of this season are internalization and introspection. The traditional objects of this season are the cauldron and the dark mirror. The cauldron represents the entrance to the Underworld, and the dark mirror symbolizes looking inward. For a simple dark mirror you can apply black paint to the underside of a clear piece of glass.

On your altar place two black candles at the opposite end from where you will be positioned. The candles should be several inches apart, and from your perspective will be to your left and right. These candles serve as the symbols of the Otherworld. In the center of your altar place the cauldron and mirror. Set a black votive candle in front of them.

The altar can be decorated with other traditional symbols such as dried leaves and gourds. Leave room for a ritual bell, which is placed on the right side of the altar. The final item needed is a small plate for offerings of cereal grains.

When you are ready to begin, light the altar candles from left to right. Ring the altar bell three times, then recite the following:

I call to the Goddess and the God to bless this ritual
on this sacred day of entering into the shadows.

Next, ring the bell three times, light the votive candle, and
say:

In the names of the God and Goddess, I call to the
spirit of quiet shadowed places. Come, partake of
the offerings I freely give here upon this altar. Grant
the inner vision and the clarity of discernment. And
through this may I gain enlightenment in the places
of darkness.

On a piece of parchment write a situation in your life that
needs either rethinking or greater discernment/meditation. You
can also write down anything that you want to be rid of in your
life, such as smoking or some other addiction. When completed,
speak your intention, fold the parchment three times, and then
drop it into the cauldron. Finally, place the dark mirror over the
cauldron like a lid.

The final phase of the ritual turns now to giving offerings to
the God and Goddess. Before presenting the offerings, say:

God and Goddess, I thank you for your presence in
my life, and for the shadows and dark periods that
help me change and grow. May your blessings of
peaceful withdrawal and contemplative solitude permeate the coming season. Please accept this offering
as a token of my love.

Place your hands, palms up, one on each side of the offering
plate as a welcome. Once the offering phase is completed you
can remove the altar items. Take the piece of parchment, soak it
in water for a few minutes, and then bury it several inches deep
in some soil.

Full Moon Ritual

Prepare an altar with a black cloth and two white altar candles (placed in the same manner as the Sabbat altar candles). Between these candles place your deity images (Goddess on the left, God on the right). Next, place your four primary ritual tools on the altar in the following pattern: pentacle (top/north position), wand (right/east position), athame (bottom/south position), chalice (left/west position). Set each tool several inches inward from the edge of the altar, and arrange them in a circular pattern. Place a bowl of clear water on the altar where it is easily reached.

Decorate your altar with seasonal flowers and other corresponding symbols of your choosing. Set a plate of sweet cookies or cakes on the altar. Pour some wine into the chalice and light some incense (jasmine or wisteria is a good choice). Extinguish all artificial lights, and then light the altar candles. You are now ready to begin.

Stand before the altar and look up at the moon, and say:

> On this sacred night of the Lady, beneath the full moon, which She has placed among the stars, I give veneration. I join on this night with all who gather in the name of the Goddess.

Hold your palms out (facing away from you) and form a triangle by touching the index fingers and thumbs of both hands together. Enclose the moon in the triangle opening formed between your fingers, and recite:

> Hail and adoration unto You, O Great Lady. Hail, Goddess of the Moon, and of the Night. You have been since before the beginning, You, who caused all things to appear, Giver and Sustainer of Life, Adoration unto You.

Lower your hands (releasing the triangle) and dip the fingers of your left hand into the bowl of water. Then anoint your forehead and recite:

My lady, I pray Thee impart to me Thy Illumination.

Anoint your eyes, and recite:

And enlighten me that I may perceive more clearly all things in which I endeavor.

Anoint your heart area, and recite:

And illuminate my soul, imparting Thy essence of Purity.

Anoint your stomach and genital area by brushing your fingers down from your navel past your genitals, and then present both palms upward to the moon as you recite:

I reveal my Inner Self to Thee and ask that all be cleansed and purified within.

Place an offering of flowers to the Goddess, setting them between your ritual tools, and recite:

O Great Lady, think yet even for a moment, upon this worshipper. Beneath the Sun do people toil, and go about, and attend to all worldly affairs. But beneath the Moon, Your children dream and awaken, and draw their power. Therefore, bless me, O Great Lady, and impart to me Your mystic Light, in which I find my powers. Bless me, O Lady of the Moon.

Hold the chalice of wine up to the moon, and recite:

O Ancient Wanderer of the Dark Heavens, Mystery of the Mysteries, emanate Your sacred essence upon me as I wait below at this appointed time. Enlighten my inner mind and spirit, as do you lighten the darkness of night.

Drink from the chalice and place it back on the altar.

Place the cookies/small cakes on the pentacle, and make sure there is still wine in the chalice. Trace a crescent over the cookies/cakes and the wine with your wand, and recite:

> Blessings upon this meal, which is as my own body. For without such sustenance, I would perish from this world. Blessings upon the grain, which as seed went into the earth where deep secrets hide. And there did dance with the elements, and spring forth as flowered plant, concealing secrets strange. When you were in the ear of grain, spirits of the field came to cast their light upon you and aid you in your growth. Thus through you shall I be touched by that same race, and the mysteries hidden within you, I shall obtain even unto the last of these grains.

Trace a crescent over the wine with your athame, and recite:

> By virtue of this sacred blade, be this wine the vital essence of the Great Goddess.

Trace a crescent over the cakes with your wand, and recite:

> By virtue of this sacred wand, be this cake the vital substance of the Great God.

Lift up the pentacle and the chalice, look up at the moon, and recite:

> Through these cakes and by this wine, may the Goddess and God bless me, and give me inner strength and vision. May I come to know that within me, which is of the eternal gods. May this blessing be so, in the names of the Lord and Lady.

Eat a portion of the meal and drink some of the wine. Leave some for libations at the close of the ritual. The wine will be poured out on the soil and the cakes tossed up to the moon.

Sit now before the altar, look up at the moon, and visualize it as the Goddess appearing to you in a sphere of light. Kiss the palm of your left hand and extend it up to her. Then say:

> O Bright Lady, Queen of all Witches, hear my adoration. Hear my voice as I speak Your praises. Receive my words as they rise heavenward, when the full moon brightly shining fills the heavens with Your beauty. See me, for I come before You, and reach my hand up to You. As the full moon shines upon me, give me all Your blessings.

(pause)

> O Great Goddess of the Moon, Goddess of the Mysteries of the Moon, teach me secrets yet revealed, ancient rites of invocation, for I believe the Witches' creed. And when I seek for knowledge, I seek and find you above all others. Give me power, O Most Secret Lady, and protect me from my enemies. When my body lies resting nightly, speak to my inner spirit, teach me all Your Holy Mysteries. I believe Your ancient promise that all who seek Your Holy Presence will receive of Your wisdom.

(pause)

> Behold, O Ancient Goddess, I have come beneath the full moon at this appointed time. Now the full moon shines upon me. Hear me and recall Your Ancient Promise. Let Your Glory shine about me. Bless me, O Gracious Queen of Heaven. In your name, so be it done.

Now it is time to bless each of the primary tools by "bathing" them in moonlight. Sprinkle some water on each tool with your left hand, then hold the tool up to the moon, and turn it in the moon's light.

Before completing the ritual, a work of magic or spell casting may be performed. When you are finished, remove all the altar items and put them away. Offer libations to the earth and the moon. The celebration is now completed.

Concerning the Sacred Ritual Meal

In the religion of Witchcraft the rituals are often centered around a sacred meal. Since ancient times feasts have always been a part of celebrating. In many cases the feasts contain symbolic and religious elements associated with the food and drink. Witchcraft is no exception, and the ritual meal features a deep connection with the old European mystery traditions.

The inner symbolism of the ritual meal is connected with two essential mystery teachings of pre-Christian origin: the Grain Mysteries and the Grail Mysteries. These two mysteries share a connection to another mystery teaching known as the Fermentation Mysteries. This mystery teaching, in turn, is associated with another called the Transformation Mysteries. All of this is covered in greater detail in my previous book *The Wiccan Mysteries*, so I will not go into great depth here and now. However, a brief overview would be helpful for the purposes of this chapter.

In modern Witchcraft the sacred meal is often referred to as "cakes and wine." To avoid overlapping associations, for the purpose of this book (and for the sake of simplicity), I will refer here to the cakes as the substance of the God and to the wine as the essence of the Goddess. The cakes and wine represent the tangible elements of the qualities of the God and Goddess as expressed in Nature. From a magical perspective, the cake is called the "vital substance" of the God, and the wine is called the "vital essence" of the Goddess.

To eat the cakes and consume the wine is to transfer a portion of the quintessence of the God and Goddess into oneself.

From a metaphysical perspective this causes an alignment to take place down to the cellular level of the body. In the old mystery traditions, after one consumed the sacred meal, these words were spoken: "May you come to know that within you, which is of the eternal gods." These words addressed the core issue, which is the alignment to the divine spark within the soul that dwells within the physical body.

Traces of this ancient mystery tradition are found also in modern Catholicism where followers of this faith partake of the sacrament of communion. This involves the eating of a communion wafer and the drinking of wine from a chalice, which is meant to represent the body and blood of Jesus Christ. Unlike the ancient mystery tradition, here the meal and the drink do not reflect the masculine and feminine elements of divinity.

Libations

Following a Witchcraft ritual, any leftover wine in the chalice is poured out on the earth. This act is called a libation, and constitutes an offering. Pouring the wine on the soil is an ancient act of veneration to both the spirits of Nature and Chthonic entities. In ancient Witchcraft libations were poured out to Hecate and Proserpina.

Once libations are offered, the leftover pieces of cake are tossed up toward the moon, or the night sky in the case where no moon is visible. In ancient times, offerings tossed up to the night sky served to venerate the goddess Diana. Thus, pouring libations and tossing bits of cake was combined to honor the triformis aspects of the Goddess of Witches: Hecate, Diana, and Proserpina.

It is an ancient practice in Witchcraft to throw a kiss to the moon when making libations and offerings. This is done with the left hand, by kissing the fleshy part of the thumb near the palm, and then throwing the kiss up to the moon. By continuing this old custom in modern times the practice of Witchcraft is kept ever ancient and ever new.

Now it is time to turn to the last chapter before we part ways at the crossroads.

200

Chapter
Eleven

TWELVE

Some Parting Words

We have come now to the end of our exploration of the spirit of the Witch. Before you now is what we refer to in the Craft as "the well-worn path." Envision a golden field of grain stretching to the horizon with no signs of human civilization. A single footpath cuts into the field, extends deep into the expanse, and then completely disappears in the thick growth. Upon closer examination we find a path well worn by the footsteps of those who have walked this way since perhaps the beginning of time.

As we follow this path deep into the field, the road is sometimes smooth and at other times pitted and covered with sharp stones. There are times when the path is scarcely discernable, but still large portions of it are wide and clearly visible. It has been cleared by the explorers who tread this path long ago. Up ahead on the path we hear the voices of those who have traveled further beyond the point that we find ourselves. They sometimes call back to us, alerting us as to what to expect as we continue our own journey, and giving us some advice based upon their personal experiences walking ahead on this road.

Some say this path has no end; others say it ends and if you would continue beyond the point where others have walked, then you must clear it further yourself. Extending the path for yourself also extends it for those coming up the path behind you. Occasionally we find smaller trails leading off and away. Whether these are the signs of some successful trailblazer, or those who have lost their way, or others who have given up and left the path, is difficult to know with any degree of certainty.

When I first ventured into the Witchcraft community over thirty years ago, Witchcraft was called "The Old Religion" and was often referred to as the well-worn path. However, in the early days of the Craft in the San Diego area (circa 1969) there were few Witch shops to be found, and most of them posed as herbal supply stores. There were few teachers of the Craft that one could encounter without the "proper" connections. Books on Witchcraft, written by Witches, were extremely rare (especially those of any value).

Today the Witchcraft community is relatively in the open and most cities have a Witch Shop or New Age store. Among the great abundance of books published by those who call themselves Witches today, there are many of value to both the beginner and the intermediate reader. Teachers of the Craft can be found in most major cities, and many Craft/Pagan magazines carry ads for mail-order courses. However, this requires greater caution and more careful discernment than ever before.

As of the writing of this book there are many respected sources available as a starting place for seekers and beginners. Magazines such as *Sagewoman*, *Circle Magazine*, *PanGaia*, and *New Witch* are very popular and well-respected publications.

These particular publications are focused on the feminine aspects of the Nature religion and are aimed primarily at a female audience. On the Internet you can find a very popular networking website called "The Witches' Voice" (www.Witchvox.com). It is designed to be of value for both men and women.

Many modern chain bookstores such as Borders and Barnes & Noble have a New Age section and carry a large selection of books on Witchcraft. Small bookstores and Witch Shops also carry many books on Witchcraft and related topics. I do encourage everyone to support these small shops in order for them to remain available as a community resource. Such places offer classes on Witchcraft and serve as excellent meeting places in which to encounter others of like mind.

The well-worn path lies ahead of you, or you may have already begun walking it. There is an old saying among Witches: "When the student is ready, the teacher appears." What you will find, as well, is that many of your teachers will not be formal ones. They will instead be found among your companions on the path. In my own journey these many long years, I have found that some of my best teachers have been my own students. To quote a Vulcan: "It isn't logical, but it is often true."

Green Wisdom

As I reflect back over my days in the Craft, I fondly recall my mother's herb garden when I was a child. It was there that I learned a love for Nature and for the Old Ways. In my mother's garden I first encountered the folk magic and folklore rooted in the rich traditions of Old Europe. Here I embraced the simple truths of an old peasant system known as the Old Religion, or Witchcraft.

When working in the garden, my mother would often call me to her side when I was a child. She would point to a certain herb and say: "Did I ever tell you what we do with this one?"

This always meant that a teaching was about to begin. If I appeared distracted and failed to show her my full attention, my mother would smile and say: "Well, maybe some other time." This always signaled that the teaching was not going to take place today, no matter how much I complained and protested.

The opportunity to be taught something had now vanished as quickly as it had come. Of all the important lessons I believe I have learned in this lifetime, none were more important than this single lesson: "Be fully present in all that you do, and appreciate each opportunity that comes your way." Looking back across the years, I realize now that my mother taught me self-discipline and focus. Without this foundation I do not believe that I would ever have achieved the successes in my life that followed.

In this book I've tried to convey a sense of the Old Ways that can enrich one's life and the experience of life itself. The Old Ways teach us that we are connected to the seasons, rhythms, and cycles of Nature. In understanding this comes the knowledge that the events in our lives have reason and purpose. For nothing in Nature is a random, unrelated occurrence. When we understand that we do not master Nature, then we begin to live in "common cause" with Nature. Only by participating with Nature as one of its dependent components can we ensure our own survival as a species.

I believe that one of the initial reasons why people are attracted to Witchcraft is the promise of learning magic. Today we live in a world that seems controlled by people, organizations, and events outside of our influence. The art of magic suggests that you and I have the tools to change this situation, and indeed we do.

Magic is the art of attracting energy, focusing it upon one's desire, and then directing both into manifesting within one's life. Every human being possesses this ability because we all possess within us the divine spark of that which created us. Think about that for a moment, and you will realize that you are the off-spring of what created the Universe! Therefore at the very center of your being resides a core that is part you and part of that which created you. This connects you directly with the divine source of all things.

For Witches, the realization of our living connection to Nature and divinity is an empowering part of Witchcraft. In my mother's garden I observed the changing seasons, and in this I beheld the changing seasons of my own existence. I learned that merging with the forces of Nature enhanced my magical abilities.

Just as in Nature, the cycle of Spring leads to Summer, so too did the energy of desire lead to the fruit of that desire, if planted and cared for properly. As a Witch, I soon discovered that ritually planting my desires at the time of the Spring Equinox leads to harvesting them in the Fall Equinox. Whatever I wish to remove from my life, I ritually release at the Fall Equinox. Winter decays it and turns its essence into raw renewed energy for the next Spring planting.

In your own seasons to come, you can see the patterns and embrace them through the spirit of the Witch. Remember always that you have the ability to tap into the natural forces that maintain the harmony of the creative elements. This is the very fabric of creation, and with it you hold the potential to make your life anything you want it to be.

Some Shared Thoughts

In this section I have placed a collection of what might be called "mini-teachings" gathered by my students over the years. These arose from conversations that were recorded as well as from emails between my students and myself. The students extracted certain phrases that had meant a great deal to them in their lives at the time for a variety of reasons. One day I was very honored to be presented with an assortment of my own "sayings" that had been collected by some of my students.

I have been encouraged to share these observations here in this book. These words seemed to have touched the spirit of certain Witches, and if one would know something of the spirit of the Witch, what better source than the Witches themselves. I hope that you will find something of value in these words as well.

Observations Along the Path

- When we cling to the negative past, we fight against phantoms, fabrics of our limited perceptions. When we bathe in the recollection of past victories and achievements, we embrace merely the pleasant fragrance of an empty perfume bottle. Whatever they have left us are frail things of the past. In one brief moment we can lose it all (good or bad). Therefore, now is all that matters. What we do today with our lives, and with our thoughts, and with our feelings is all that really matters.

- To be a Witch is to understand that we have the power to shape things and to decide how we will, or will not, react to the environment around us. This is because everything is "Mind." We can become its servant or we can become its director. We can listen to it describe how things are (or were), or we can tell it how it is, and how it's going to be.

- It is important to understand that life is not like ordering fast food from Jack-in-the-Box. You can't always get fries, and a drink, and a hamburger, and an apple pie. Often, all we can get is a meal "sorta-kinda-like" what we had in mind. But hey, it's food. It's really a waste of precious energy to grieve over what we don't have instead of taking advantage of what we can achieve. In reality all we actually have is this very moment. So what are you going to do with it now? Yesterday is just a memory, good or bad.

Tomorrow is just a promise, colored by our mindset. The only thing we can really do anything about is right now.

- When the voice we accept reminds us of our failures, we need to forgive ourselves for our weaknesses and our mistakes. If we were perfect, we would not be dwelling in the Physical Dimension. We are here to learn lessons, and to gain wisdom and compassion from them.

- When we injure a foot, it is painful to keep walking on it. We need to give it a rest. We need to acknowledge that we have injured ourselves. Then we need to modify our behavior and allow the injury to heal. Pain is Nature's way of saying "stop doing that." So, too, it is with emotional pain. It serves its purpose, but it does not allow healing if we continue to stimulate the pain. We have to replace the stimulation with the affirmation to heal: "Yes, I injured my foot, it was stupid, but now I am going to rest it and heal." Then we take steps to not repeat what led to the injury in the first place. If we continue to repeat the steps that resulted in the injury, then we are listening to a voice that dictates, rather than one that guides us. It is up to us.

- Trust that balance is assured in this life. In the Winter it is useless to rage against the cold. Take what warmth is available, participate as is appropriate to the season, and await the renewal that is always guaranteed with the coming of Spring.

- The joys and sorrows of this life help weave the patterns of light and darkness, which become the colors and designs that mark us in our "butterfly" emergence into another type of existence.

- Asking why is not as important as simply dealing with it. Essentially, most of the things in our lives we bring to ourselves. But, we do have the power to decide how we will deal with it, how we will react to it, and how we will feel about it (that is, after the initial shock). Remember, we are not victims of the Universe. We are weavers and shapers. Take the stuff that gets dumped on you and re-fashion it into something more desirable. It's your choice; be a victim or a fashion designer.

- What the gods don't transform through fire in us, we seem to set fire to ourselves. In a mythical sense, "hell" or "purgatory" is a state of mind in which one burns with negative emotional fire. But as Witches, when we've had enough pain, we remove our hand from the fire.

- Deity is with you, your power animal is with you, spirits are with you, and your ancestors are with you. Sometimes we need to listen for the answer when we ask for the aid. Internal dialogue is like a busy phone line. Running off, trying to fix every problem for every person is like not being home when the important phone call comes in (and having forgotten to put the answering machine on).

- The Universe is full of surprises. When we're on a roller coaster, it is always best to simply hold on to the bar and stay focused on keeping our place inside. The ride is the ride, whether enjoyable or not, but in its own time it comes to a stop. Then we have the choice of getting back in line, or never going on it again.

- The core issue is that we are spiritual beings having a human experience. The purpose of life is to prepare the soul for the realm in which it is intended to dwell. To ac-complish that the soul must learn compassion. To learn compassion one must be set free from judgment. To be set free from judgment one must see others as they see themselves. To see others as one sees oneself, one must look at the indwelling soul. In looking at the indwelling soul one will discover another soul who is having a hu-man experience also. In this mirror one will see one's twin. In seeing one's twin, one will see oneself. Seeing oneself in others allows one to correct his or her own condition. Correction frees one judgment, for correction resolves, but judgment only maintains. Therefore, in the end, we must discern and ask what is the correct thing to do? This is how we make the soul's choice, by always doing what is right, especially when we wish not to.

- Have you ever pondered the difference between a person who is filled with the spirit of Divinity and one who is filled simply with their own spirit? Both can appear to have joy and both can speak of lofty things. The difference is only clear when this person is alone, with no one else around for them to impress or give false impressions to. I guess that's why the way to the answers lies within.

- So many folks are looking for a short cut to enlightenment without having to do any of the work, but self-discipline and effort are part of what elevates us to enlightenment to begin with!

- Compassion comes from our understanding of pain. Pain is a purifier and helps to forge our spirit as a tool for others to benefit by. Knowing this does not make it less painful, but it does give it purpose.

- Take the gifts that are offered in whatever way they are offered. Despair is often born of our fears. Fear is born from our own insecurities. Trust that the Universe is "unfolding as it should" and that you are not a victim of it, but rather a participant in its patterns of light and darkness. I would suggest that you take pause and affirm the light in your life. Sit quietly and visualize yourself engulfed in a bright white light. Say aloud:

> I am surrounded by the purity of divine light. Nothing but good shall come to me, nothing but good shall come from me.

Repeat this over several times. It is also good to have a light and pleasant incense burning while performing this.

Above all, you must realize that you are not a victim in this life, but rather a conscious participant in it. People and things are only catalysts to our feelings, but they cannot make us feel one way or the other. We have the power over how we feel, how we perceive, and how we react. The choice must be made as to whether we allow someone else, or something else, to be responsible for how we feel or whether we ourselves make the conscious decision.

- You know that for every action there is a reaction. Therefore what is in your life you bring to your life. If you are unhappy with your life, then act upon it.

- Fears can present us with problems and confuse us concerning actions we should take, or not take. But even making the wrong choices can help us to grow as a spiritual being. Oddly enough, making the right choice is not always without pain and we can be afraid even to do what is right. But if doing right was always easy, then it would become a mundane thing and would lose its distinction.

- It is the purpose of a guide to point a person to the source of enlightenment and then stand by to help if needed. If a person doesn't get it, then the guide can point out either another approach or suggest trying the same one again. You never walk alone, even when you feel you are.

- To uncover our divine nature is to begin to understand who we are and why we are. After that, we must do something about it.

- Human experiences weave a pattern of light and darkness in our lives. We cannot define something without its opposite. If we knew nothing of the cold we would not know what it means to be warm. Much of our strength comes from the past adversity we have experienced. It is here also that the roots of compassion lie. You cannot be who you are and who you were meant to be without the light and darkness of your life experience. Therefore, embrace the blessings of light and darkness, for they have made you unique. Uniqueness is one of the vital contributions you get to make in this world.

Where to Now?

Several years ago, shortly after the publication of my first book, I received a phone call from one of my aunts living in Pennsylvania whom I had not spoken with in many years. Her name is Dolly and she is from the side of my family that is German and Scottish. She called to congratulate me on the publication of my book, and during the course of our conversation Dolly revealed something to me that I had not previously known.

According to Dolly, my uncle Frank and my grandmother (both now deceased) had been Pennsylvania Dutch hex folk. My uncle reportedly performed healings with cigar smoke, and my grandmother diagnosed illness by examining the feathers inside a patient's bedroom pillow. She went on describing various things my grandmother and uncle did as practitioners. Following this she said, "Yeah, they could have told you a lot of things," and then she fell silent for a moment. When she spoke again, Dolly said, "But there isn't anyone left now to tell you anything."

I felt a profound sense of sadness in hearing my aunt's words. The idea that a school of knowledge simply vanished with the passing of two individuals left me with a feeling of true loss. There are certain things disappearing in our world that we will probably not be able to save. I would hate to think that knowledge is one of those things.

Today there are two schools of Witchcraft. One is rooted in pre-Christian European religion and contains the old mystery concepts that once flourished and now largely reside in the shadows of myth and legend. Such systems contain traditional concepts constructed around ancestral knowledge, wisdom, and experience. The other school emerged in the early 1980s (although rooted in the work of Gerald Gardner, circa 1954) and is constructed around self-styled, self-adapted, and eclectic views mixed with an intuitive approach.

Although this demonstrates a fork in the road for practical purposes, both paths can still be explored or combined. In the appendices that follow I have compiled a list of books into categories that I believe will be helpful in the study and research of Witchcraft as a religion and a spiritual path. This will provide the beginner with a basic course of study, which will guide him or her along the well-worn path. I encourage everyone to preserve the old knowledge contained within Witchcraft before it completely disappears beneath the wave of modern transformation.

For further information and study opportunities, contact College of the Crossroads, P. O. Box 2315, Valley Center, California 92082, or www.collegeofthecrossroads.org

A Word to the Wise

Before closing the book, I think it is important to say a few things concerning one of the fast-growing modern influences on the Witchcraft community. What I refer to here is the Internet chat rooms and discussion boards. If you have a computer you can access a variety of chat rooms and discussion boards hosted on various websites. The purpose of these forums is to provide a place for people to exchange information, engage in healthy debates, create networks, and establish online communities. Many friendships have begun by "meeting" online.

The majority of the chat rooms and discussion boards are frequented by seekers and beginners, as well as by some more seasoned and experienced individuals in the Craft community. Most of the people you will meet are sincere folks with good common sense. However, there are others whose motives for being a member are suspect, and whose integrity and knowledge seems questionable. Such individuals, although claiming to be Witches, don't behave as would best befit a Witch in a public forum. Unfortunately these individuals are also commonly among the most vocal members in the chat rooms and on the discussion boards.

Today we have this wonderful opportunity to communicate with one another, to share, and engage in healthy and productive debate. Through this we can all be enriched in many ways. But I've found from personal experience that a small minority of people want to spend their time (and the time that others have online) with little more than mean-spirited postings and spiteful remarks. I would suggest that time is all too precious, and should not be wasted in this way. There is so much opportunity for information, camaraderie, and growth here, that it seems healthiest to nurture that instead of encouraging negativity.

A discernment of spirit is always a helpful thing. People who spend their time degrading others may not be people who you want to get to know you very well. People who openly display hostility, hate, disrespect, and intolerance may not be people you wish to embrace as teachers and companions in the Craft. It may be more beneficial for you to not encourage such individuals by responding, and instead devote your time to dialogue with people who practice common courtesy and are respectful of others.

You will encounter disagreements in any chat room or discussion board. Respectful differences are helpful in revealing different perspectives, which is beneficial in allowing us to see the many sides of any one issue. Name-calling, rudeness, haughtiness, and condescension are often signs of emotional immaturity. The views of such individuals may not be the best and most reliable ones upon which to form an agreement.

My best advice is to simply speak your own truths without ostentation. Avoid discussions involving character assassination and any general bashing of others, as it is usually just the ranting of people who are unhappy with their own lives. Devote your time instead to people who seem balanced, thoughtful, friendly, and helpful. This is a much more productive use of your time, and will help you sort out the true Witches from those who "talk the talk" but don't "walk the walk" of our path.

Parting at the Crossroads

Throughout the course of this book we have looked at the spirit of the Witch in a variety of forms. Hopefully in revealing the true inner beauty of the Witch, the false ugliness has now vanished. I am hopeful that this book has helped to dispel the negative stereotypes concerning Witches, and will continue to serve as an aid to understanding and acceptance.

It is time now for us to part ways as this book comes to its conclusion. It is fitting to say that we have come to the fork in the road, the crossroad of our journey together. In ancient times the crossroad was sacred to the goddess Hecate because of its *triformis* nature. The ancient concept of a crossroad was where three roads meet, rather than the common modern concept of a "four-way" stop.

The classic crossroad is "Y" shaped and symbolizes past, present and future. It also represents the serpent's forked tongue, which symbolizes the transformative power of the snake to shed its dead skin, move on, and continue to grow. The snake uses its tongue to "taste" the air and to discern what it senses in the surrounding environment. The choices made by the snake then direct its movement.

Hecate is a goddess who brings changes to our lives because she calls on us to make a decision. She leads us to many crossroads in our life, and then holds her torches to cast light on the road that stands divided at our feet. Hecate does not tell us which way to go; she merely provides the light in which we can discern our choice. Perhaps reading this book has brought you to the crossroads as well.

NOTES

Chapter Two

1. Grimassi, Raven. *The Witches' Craft* (Llewellyn Worldwide Ltd., St. Paul, Minn., 2002).

2. Lattimore, Richmond. *Hesiod: The Works and Days, Theogony, and The Shields of Herakles* (University of Michigan Press, Ann Arbor, Mich., 1959).

3. Ibid.

4. Grimassi, 2002.

5. Lambardo, Stanley, and Karen Bell. *Protagoras* (Indianapolis: Hackett Publishing Co., 1992).

6. Frazer, James. *Myths of the Origin of Fire* (London, 1930).

7. Neumann, Erich. *The Great Mother: An Analysis of the Archetype* (Princeton University Press, Princeton, Mass., 1974).

8. Falassi, Alessandro. *Folklore by the Fireside: Text and Context of the Tuscan Veglia* (University of Texas Press, Austin, Tex., 1980).

9. Manciocco, Claudia and Luigi. *Una Casa Senza Porte* (Melusina Editrice, Rome, 1995).

10. Frazer, James. *The Golden Bough* (MacMillan Company, New York, 1951).

11. Neumann.

12. Ibid.

13. Purkiss, Diane. *The Witch in History* (Routledge, London, 1996).

14. Lattimore.

15. Neumann.

Chapter Three

1. *Lunario Toscana,* in Hazlitt, W. C. *Dictionary of Faiths & Folklore* (London: Bracken Books, 1995).

2. *De Temporum Ratione,* in Hazlitt.

3. Gimbutas, Marija. *The Goddesses and Gods of Old Europe* (University of California Press, Berkeley, Calif., 1982).

4. Hazlitt.

5. Tolkien, J. R. R. *The Return of the King* (New York: Houghton Mifflin, 1988).

6. Starhawk. *The Spiral Dance: A Rebirth of the Ancient Religion of the Great Goddess* (HarperSanFrancisco, 1999).

7. Frazer, 1951.

Chapter Five

1. Gordon, Richard. "Imagining Greek and Roman Magic," in Ankarloo and Clark's *Witchcraft and Magic in Europe: Ancient Greece and Rome* (University of Pennsylvania Press, 1999).

2. Leland, Charles G. *Aradia: Gospel of the Witches* (Samuel Weiser Inc., New York, 1974).

Chapter Seven

1. Turcan, Robert. *The Cults of the Roman Empire* (Blackwell, Cambridge, Mass., 1996).

Chapter Eight

1. Grimassi, Raven. *Wiccan Magick* [1998], and *The Witches' Craft* [1998] (Llewellyn Worldwide Ltd., St. Paul, Minn.).

Chapter Nine

1. Lattimore.

2. Sheba, Lady. *The Grimoire of Lady Sheba* (St. Paul: Llewellyn Worldwide Ltd., 1972).

3. Gardner, Gerald. *Witchcraft Today* (Citadel Press, New York, 1973).

4. Leland, Charles G. *Etruscan Roman Remains* (T. Fisher Unwin, London, 1892).

5. Lattimore.

6. Ibid.

Chapter Ten

1. Guazzo, Francesco Maria. *Compendium Maleficarum* (Dover, New York, 1988).

2. Cavendish, Richard. *The Powers of Evil* (New York: G. P. Putnam's Sons, 1975).

3. Grimassi, Raven. *The Wiccan Mysteries* (Llewellyn Worldwide Ltd., St. Paul, Minn., 1997).

Chapter Eleven

1. Campbell, Joseph. *The Hero with a Thousand Faces* (Princeton: Princeton University Press, 1973).

Training Exercises

The art of Witchcraft requires the development of strong visualization abilities and powers of concentration. Concentration can be strengthened through meditation. The ability of a Witch to visualize and focus his or her concentration with distraction is essential in the performance of magic. As noted in previous chapters, personal will is also an important component.

Visualization Exercise

Draw a star figure and color it in with a bright yellow highlighter pen or colored pencil. In other words, the full body of the star will be solid yellow. The star should be about one to two inches tall (see p. 220). When the star is colored, fix your gaze directly on the center of the star. Stare at it as you count slowly to the number ninety.

You may use this star as a template for making the yellow star for the visualization exercise.

When you are finished counting, look quickly at a blank white piece of paper (computer paper works well) and keep your gaze fixed (do not look around). In a moment a blue star will appear on the paper. If you close your eyes you should also be able to "see" the blue star.

Repeat this exercise several times over the next two or three days (but not on one day in succession). This will fix the image of the blue star firmly in your memory. The next phase is to try to *see* the blue star against a white background without using the yellow star. In effect, you will be trying to recall the image in your mind's eye. With time and attentive practice, you should be able to reproduce the visualized blue star.

Once you are successful, then try using other images as a focal point, and afterward concentrate on reproducing them in your mind's eye. When you can "see" an object at will through visualization, then you are at a sufficient level to apply your ability to magical intents.

Concentration Exercise

The ability to concentrate can be strengthened by focusing the mind on a simple figure or design. The traditional figures are the triangle, circle, square, crescent, and oval. Draw one of the symbols on a piece of paper or trace one from the illustration below, and then concentrate on it for a few moments. Then try to visualize the figure in your mind's eye. Your goal is to be able to *see* the image with your mind and then maintain it for one minute.

Once you have mastered one of the images move on to the next. When you have mastered the five figures you will have achieved the level necessary to apply your ability to works of magic. For an advance technique, color the images and try visualizing them in their color. The traditional color assignments are: square (yellow), circle (blue), triangle (red), crescent (silver), and oval (black).

Symbols for use in Concentration Exercises.

Witches' Altars

This section will provide you with some altar layouts that are more symbolic and involved than the ones described in various chapters of the book. Witches often use different types of altars for different purposes. The following are some examples you can use.

For Ritual

Lay the altar pentacle directly centered on the altar. Next place elemental bowls around the pentacle to symbolize the creative elemental substances from which all things are created: Earth, Air, Fire, Water. The bowl representing Earth is set in the North position and contains sand, small stones, or salt. To the East, place the elemental bowl containing incense (smoking) to represent Air, and to the

South a bowl with a red votive candle for Fire. In the Western placement is a bowl of purified Water.

The ritual wand is placed off to the Eastern edge of the altar. The ritual dagger is placed at the Southern edge. The chalice is set near the Western edge of the altar. You will note that the pentacle is not at the Northern edge, but rather in the center of the altar. This is because here the pentacle represents the physical plane, the focal point of the ritual energy. Mundane tools such as a utility knife, candle snuffer, and so on, may be placed in the southern section of the altar for easy reach. With this arrangement the ritual altar is now complete.

For Spell Work

Lay the altar pentacle toward the upper edge and centered side-to-side on the altar. Set a metallic bowl (spirit bowl) containing a flammable liquid such as perfume or liqueur, directly centered on the altar. This liquid will burn with a beautiful blue flame, representing the presence of Divinity. In place of the fluid you can burn a candle in a blue glass container. Next, place elemental bowls around the center bowl or blue glass candleholder (the creative elemental substances from which all things are made manifest). These bowls contain representations of the four elements: Earth, Air, Fire, and Water. The bowl representing Earth is set in the North position and contains salt. To the East, lay the bowl containing incense (smoking) to represent Air, to the South set a bowl with a red votive candle for Fire, and to the West is placed a bowl of purified Water.

The ritual wand is set next to the Air elemental bowl. The ritual dagger is placed near the elemental votive candle, and the chalice by the bowl of Water. Mundane tools such as a utility knife, candle snuffer, and so on, may be placed at the North. With this arrangement the altar is now complete.

For Blessing Objects

This type of altar is used to consecrate ritual tools, amulets, personal jewelry, or anything that you want to treat as special. In the center of the altar place a medium-size bowl of purified water. Brew a tea made of the following herbs: rosemary, hyssop, and acacia. Then pour this blend of herbs into the bowl. Add three small pinches of salt to the mixture. When blessing personal jewelry you can also add three drops of your favorite perfume to the concoction. This will help to make the alignment unique to yourself.

It is good to place a statue of the God and Goddess on the altar to represent the meeting point with divinity as you perform blessings. Hold the object being blessed up to each divine image and ask for blessings in the name of your Goddess and God. A cowrie shell or moonstone can be placed on your altar to connect with the essence of the Goddess. A piece of stag horn, goat horn, or bull horn can be set on the altar to align with the essence of the God.

Place four small bowls near the lower portion of the altar, forming an equilateral cross. These will be your elemental bowls. In the top bowl, pour some salt. In the right bowl, place some mint leaves. In the bottom bowl set a red votive candle. In the left bowl, pour some clean water. In the center between the bowls, place a small container of burning incense; dragon's blood incense works very well.

To bless an object, dip it into the center bowl of water. Then present the object to each of the deity images. Next, touch the object to each of the elemental bowls. End by passing the object through the dragon's blood incense. The symbolism of this is as follows. The water represents birth. Presenting the object to the deity statues symbolizes the bonding of parent to magickal child. Touching the object to each elemental bowl empowers the alignment of the creative elements that provide the vital essence. Conclude by passing the object through the incense smoke, which symbolizes that the blessing is made in harmony with the spirit that binds the four elements together.

Appendix
Two

Suggested Course Reading

The following list of books will provide you with a solid foundation in understanding the basic structure of the Craft, its tenets, practices, and rituals.

Category One: Foundation

The Witches' Way: Principles, Rituals, and Beliefs of Modern Witchcraft by Janet and Stewart Farrar. Robert Hale, 1984.

Eight Sabbats for Witches by Janet and Stewart Farrar. Robert Hale, 1981.

Witchcraft from the Inside by Ray Buckland. Llewellyn Worldwide Ltd., 1995.

Witchcraft Today by Gerald Gardner. Citadel Press, 1973.

The Meaning of Witchcraft by Gerald Gardner. Samuel Weiser, 1976.

The Rebirth of Modern Witchcraft by Doreen Valiente. Robert Hale, 1989.

Witchcraft: A Tradition Renewed by Doreen Valiente and Evan Jones. Phoenix Publications Inc., 1990.

Witchcraft for Tomorrow by Doreen Valiente. St. Martin's Press, 1978.

The Secrets of Ancient Witchcraft, with the Witches' Tarot by Arnold and Patricia Crowther. University Books, Inc., 1974.

Category Two: Religion & Spirituality

A Witch Alone by Marian Green. Aquarian Press, 1991.

Wicca, The Old Religion in the New Age by Vivianne Crowley. Aquarian Press, 1989.

The Philosophy of Witchcraft by Ian Ferguson. George G. Harrap & Co. Ltd., 1924.

The Great Mother by Erich Neumann. Princeton University Press, 1974.

The Wiccan Mysteries by Raven Grimassi. Llewellyn Publications, 1997.

Woman's Mysteries: Ancient & Modern by M. Esther Harding. Shambala, 1990.

Category Three: The Mystery Tradition

The Underworld Initiation by R. J. Stewart. Aquarian Press, 1985.

Power Within the Land by R. J. Stewart. Element, 1994.

Western Inner Workings by William Gray. Samuel Weiser, 1983.

The Roebuck in the Thicket by Evan John Jones and Robert Cochrane. Capall Bann Publishing, 2001.

Witchcraft, A Tradition Renewed by Doreen Valiente and Evan Jones. Phoenix Publishing Inc., 1990.

Category Four: Related Studies

Wiccan Roots: Gerald Gardner and the Modern Witchcraft Revival by Philip Heselton. Capall Bann Publishing, 2000.

The Cauldron of Change: Myths, Mysteries and Magick of the Goddess by De-Anna Alba. Delphi Press, 1993.

The Spiral Dance: A Rebirth of the Ancient Religion of the Great Goddess by Starhawk. HarperSanFrancisco, 1999.

The Mysteries of Britain: The Secret Rites and Traditions of Ancient Britain Restored by Lewis Spence. New Castle Publishing, 1993.

Magic Arts in Celtic Britain by Lewis Spence. Aquarian Press, 1970.

The Fairy Tradition in Britain by Lewis Spence. Kessinger Publishing Company, n.d.

Category Five: Classic Works

The White Goddess by Robert Graves. Farrar, Straus and Giroux, 1974.

The Golden Bough by James G. Frazer. MacMillan Company, 1951.

Witches: The investigation of an ancient religion involving the worship of Diana—the Witch Cult—laying as much stress on the consorts of the goddess and on the lady herself by T. C. Lethbridge. Citadel Press, 1962.

The Witch-Cult in Western Europe by Margaret A. Murray. Barnes & Noble, 1996.

The God of the Witches by Margaret A. Murray. Oxford University Press, 1952.

GLOSSARY

Agrarian: Concerning agriculture and the cultivation of land. A farming community and the beliefs and practices of such groups.

Air: One of the four elements of creation. The elemental principle of expansion and movement. The spiritual quality of the mind and of thoughts.

Astral Plane: The realm in which "thoughts become things." Here magic takes root as thoughts are formed into cohesive visual representations. Once rooted, the energy causes a material replica to form within the material dimension.

Chthonic: A reference to deities and spirits of the Underworld. The word is derived from the Greek *khthonios* (of the earth) and *khthon* (from the earth).

Circe: In ancient Greek and Roman writings Circe was a sorceress and a Witch. One of her earliest tales appears in Homer's Odyssey.

Diana: A Roman goddess similar to the Greek Artemis. In classical Witchcraft, Diana was one of the three aspects of Hecate. In her earliest cult she was worshipped as a mother goddess, and then later as a deity who aided childbirth. Eventually she was simply depicted as a moon goddess and a deity presiding over wild game of the forest and woodlands.

Earth: One of the four elements of creation. The principle of cohesion, stability, and fortitude. The spiritual quality of solidarity.

Elemental Plane: One of the seven planes of manifestation. The dimension of creativity and the etheric qualities of Earth, Air, Fire, and Water.

Elemental Spirits: The beings that work and live in the elemental realm. Spirits known as Gnomes, Sylphs, Salamanders, and Undines. The spirits of Earth, Air, Fire, and Water.

Etheric: A nonphysical, vaporous-like substance, a spiritual essence in energy form.

Fire: One of the four elements of creation. The principle of transformation, vitality, and stimulus. The spiritual quality of motivation and energizing.

Hecate: A Greek goddess originally portrayed as one of the Elder Titan deities who existed before the Olympic gods.

Hesiod: A Greek poet who lived in the eighth century B.C.E. He is famous for his writings: *Works and Days*, and his *Theogony*, which provided the first written record of the Aegean/ Mediterranean bardic tales concerning the gods and the beginning of the world.

Homer: A Greek epic poet who lived around 850 B.C.E. He is famous for his works, the *Iliad* and the *Odyssey*.

Horace: A Roman lyric poet of the first century B.C.E. He is famous for his work *The Epodes*, among many others. His writings had a major influence on English poetry.

Iconography: The pictorial representation of an object such as a drawing or statue. A set of specific symbolic forms that are associated with a particular theme related to an image.

Lucan: A Roman poet of the first century C.E.

Medea: A Witch who appears in classical Witchcraft literature as a powerful sorceress and priestess of the Goddess Hecate.

Ovid: A Roman poet (43 B.C.E.–17 C.E.) famous for his work titled *Metamorphoses* (among others).

Pantheon: The gods and goddesses that are unique to a specific culture or group of people.

Paracelsus: A German-Swiss alchemist of the fourteenth century.

Plane: A dimension in time and space. In occult tradition there are seven planes that comprise all of existence: Ultimate, Divine, Spiritual, Mental, Astral, Elemental, and Physical.

Plato: A Greek philosopher and student of Socrates. He lived in Greece and founded the Academy some time around 386 B.C.E.

Poppet: A small image usually made of cloth, and fashioned in the image of a person with the intent of placing an enchantment on the individual. The doll is stuffed with symbolic herbs and usually contains a lock of hair or some fingernail clippings from the individual whose likeness it depicts.

Proserpina: A Roman goddess similar to the Greek Persephone. In classical Witchcraft, Proserpina was one of the three aspects of Hecate. In her earliest cult she was seen as an Underworld goddess, and then later as a moon goddess presiding over departed souls.

Pythagoras: A Greek philosopher and mathematician of the sixth century B.C.E. A Mystery School was established by his followers in southern Italy at Crotona, and the pentagram ring became a symbol of this sect.

Triformis: Having a triple nature, being comprised of three forms or aspects.

Watchers: A spiritual fellowship of guardians once believed to have existed in material form. They have long since evolved into spiritual beings and are the basis for legends regarding angels, spirit guides, and various "Otherworld" beings.

Water: One of the four elements of creation. The principle of mutability, dissolution, and motion. The spiritual quality of adaptation and of emotion.

BIBLIOGRAPHY

Adler, Margot. *Drawing Down the Moon: Witches, Druids, Goddess-Worshippers, & Other Pagans in America Today.* New York: Viking Press, 1979.

Alba, De-Anna. *The Cauldron of Change: Myths, Mysteries and Magick of the Goddess.* Oak Park: Delphi Press, Inc., 1993.

Anderson, Graham. *Fairytale in the Ancient World.* London: Routledge, 2000.

Ankarloo, Bengt, and Stuart Clark. *Witchcraft and Magic in Europe: Ancient Greece and Rome.* Philadelphia: University of Pennsylvania Press, 1999.

Baring, A., and J. Cashford. *The Myth of the Goddess: Evolution of an Image.* London: Arkana Press, 1993.

Beck, Adams L. *The Way of Power: Studies in the Occult.* New York: Cosmopolitan Corp., 1928.

Berger, Helen A. *A Community of Witches: Contemporary Neo-Paganism and Witchcraft in the United States.* Columbia: University of South Carolina Press, 1999.

Bergman, Charles. *Orion's Legacy: A Cultural History of Man as Hunter.* New York: Dutton, 1996.

Bord, Janet and Colin. *Earth Rites: Fertility Practices in Pre-Industrial Britain.* London: Granada Publishing Ltd., 1982.

Breslaw, Elaine G. *Witches of the Atlantic World.* New York: New York University Press, 2000.

Briggs, Katharine. *The Vanishing People: Fairy Lore and Legends.* New York: Pantheon Books, 1978.

Briggs, Robin. *Witches & Neighbors: The Social and Cultural Context of European Witchcraft.* New York: Viking, 1996.

Campbell, Joseph. *Primitive Mythology: The Masks of God.* New York: Arkana, 1991.

Canepa, Nancy L. *Out of the Woods: The Origins of the Literary Fairy Tale in Italy and France.* Detroit: Wayne State University Press, 1997.

Carpenter, Edward. *The Origins of Pagan and Christian Beliefs.* London: Senate, 1996.

Davies, Morganna, and Aradia Lynch. *Keepers of the Flame: Interviews with Elders of Traditional Witchcraft in America.* Providence: Olympian Press, 2001.

Dumezil, Georges. *Archaic Roman Religion.* Baltimore and London: Johns Hopkins University Press, 1996.

Evans-Wentz, W. Y. *The Fairy Faith in Celtic Countries.* New York: Carol Publishing Group, 1994.

Falassi, Alessandro. *Folklore by the Fireside: Text and Context of the Tuscan Veglia.* Austin: University of Texas Press, 1980.

Farrar, Janet and Stewart. *The Witches' Way: Principles, Rituals and Beliefs of Modern Witchcraft.* London: Robert Hale, 1984.

Fortune, Dion. *Aspects of Occultism.* Wellingborough: Aquarian Press, 1973.

Frazer, James G. *Myths of the Origin of Fire.* London: Trinity College Press, 1930.

Gardner, Gerald B. *Witchcraft Today.* Secaucus, N. J.: Citadel Press, 1973.

George, Demetra. *Mysteries of the Dark Moon.* New York: HarperCollins, 1992.

Gimbutas, Marija. *The Goddesses and Gods of Old Europe.* Berkeley: University of California Press, 1982.

Green, Marian. *A Witch Alone.* London: Aquarian Press, 1991.

Greenwood, Susan. *Magic, Witchcraft and the Otherworld.* New York: Berg, 2000.

Griffyn, Sally. *Wiccan Wisdom Keepers: Modern Witches Speak on Environmentalism, Feminism, Motherhood, Wiccan Lore, and More.* Boston: Weiser Books, 2002.

Guazzo, Francesco Maria. *Compendium Maleficarum.* New York: Dover, 1988.

Harding, M. Esther. *Woman's Mysteries: Ancient & Modern.* Boston: Shambala, 1990.

Hazlitt, W. C. *Dictionary of Faiths & Folklore.* London: Bracken Books, 1995.

Hutton, Ronald. *The Triumph of the Moon: A History of Modern Pagan Witchcraft.* New York: Oxford University Press, 1999.

Johnston, Sarah Iles. *Hekate Soteira: A Study of Hekate's Roles in the Chaldean Oracles and Related Literature.* Atlanta: Scholar's Press, 1990.

Kerenyi, Carl. *Dionysos: Archetypal Image of Indestructible Life.* Princeton: Princeton University Press, 1976.

Kingsley, Peter. *Ancient Philosophy, Mystery, and Magic.* Oxford: Oxford University Press, 1995.

Lattimore, Richmond. *Hesiod: The Works and Days, Theogony, and The Shields of Herakles.* Ann Arbor: University of Michigan Press, 1959.

Leland, Charles G. *Etruscan Roman Remains.* London: T. Fisher Unwin, 1892.

Luhrmann, T. M. *Persuasions of the Witch's Craft: Ritual Magic in Contemporary England*. Cambridge: Harvard University Press, 1989.

Manciocco, Claudia and Luigi. *Una Casa Senza Porte*. Rome: Melusina Editrice, 1995.

Marler, Joan, editor. *From the Realm of the Ancestors: An Anthology in Honor of Marija Gimbutas*. Manchester: Knowledge, Ideas, and Trends, Inc., 1997.

Mercatante, Anthony S. *Good and Evil in Myth & Legend*. New York: Barnes & Noble Books, 1996.

Neumann, Erich. *The Great Mother: An Analysis of the Archetype*. Princeton: Princeton University Press, 1974.

Ogden, Daniel. *Magic, Witchcraft, and Ghosts in the Greek and Roman Worlds*. New York: Oxford University Press, 2002.

O'Keefe, Daniel Lawrence. *Stolen Lightning: The Social Theory of Magic*. New York: Vintage Books, 1983.

Paine, Lauran. *Witchcraft and the Mysteries*. London: Robert Hale & Co., 1975.

Purkiss, Diane. *The Witch in History*. London: Routledge, 1996.

Rabinowitz, Jacob. *The Rotting Goddess: The Origin of the Witch in Classical Antiquity's Demonization of Fertility Religion*. Brooklyn: Autonomedia, 1998.

Sagan, Carl, and Ann Druyan. *Shadows of Forgotten Ancestors*. New York: Ballantine, 1992.

Spence, Lewis. *The Mysteries of Britain: The Secret Rites and Traditions of Ancient Britain Restored*. Van Nuys: New Castle Publishing, 1993.

Turcan, Robert. *The Cults of the Roman Empire*. Cambridge: Blackwell, 1996.

Ulansey, David. *The Origins of the Mithraic Mysteries*. New York: Oxford University Press, 1989.

Vale, V., and John Sulak. *Modern Pagans: An Investigation of Contemporary Pagan Practices*. San Francisco: RE Research, 2001.

Valiente, Doreen. *Witchcraft for Tomorrow*. New York: St. Martin's Press, 1978.

Von Rudloff, Robert. *Hekate in Ancient Greek Religion*. Victoria: Horned Owl Publishing, 1999.

Warren, Nathan B. *The Holidays: Christmas, Easter and Whitsuntide: Their Social Festivities, Customs, and Carols*. New York: Cambridge Riverside Press, 1868.

INDEX

Arrow, 77, 79

Athame, 48, 64, 88, 105–108,
111–112, 126–127, 134, 136,
194, 196

Beltane, vi, 30, 39–40, 42, 175,
178, 187

Between the Worlds, 81, 87–88,
125, 133, 145

Birds, 14–15, 39, 63, 98–99,
125, 154, 162

Broom, 12, 20, 24, 45,
114–115

Cauldron, 12, 20–23, 114, 139,
147, 179–183, 185–186,
192–193, 229, 235

Cave, 12, 17–19, 127

Cernunnos, 40, 158

Chalice, 23, 48, 64, 88, 105,
107–109, 113, 126–127,
136, 194–196, 199, 224

Child of Promise, 33, 159–160,
174, 176, 183

Cimaruta, 77–81

Cremation, 145

Death, 3, 17, 23, 29, 34–37, 45,
50, 56, 63, 70, 137–138, 145,
147, 155–157, 159, 161,
171–172, 175, 191

Devil, xi, 9–10, 27

Diana, 10, 21, 24, 71, 77, 79,
82–83, 199, 229, 231

Dionysos, 22, 158, 237

Divine Spark, 56–57, 89, 116,
142, 174, 199, 204

Elements, xii–xiv, 12, 14, 41–
42, 47–48, 53, 63– 64, 70,
106, 109, 114, 116, 121,
123–127, 139, 142, 145, 150,
159, 161–162, 173, 187, 196,
198–199, 205, 224–226,
231–232, 234

Elves, 165–166

Equinox, 29, 34, 36–38, 44–45, 64, 144, 158, 164, 169, 174–176, 178, 185, 192, 205

Fairy, 9, 16–17, 19, 80–81, 87, 114, 154, 165–167, 229, 236

Fall, 5, 7, 29, 32, 44–45, 64, 104, 107, 144, 150, 174, 181, 205

Fates, 20, 83

Fire, 12–14, 18–22, 32–33, 36, 39–40, 42, 47–48, 64, 82–83, 87, 109–112, 116, 123–124, 127, 142, 145–147, 162–163, 170, 174, 181, 183, 208, 215, 223–224, 232, 236

Gnomes, 48, 124, 162, 166, 232

God, 13, 22, 24, 28–29, 32, 37, 40–41, 44–45, 53–54, 62–65, 67–71, 77, 84–85, 92, 101, 107, 109–113, 140, 152–154, 157–161, 165, 172–176, 180–194, 196, 198, 225, 229, 236

Goddess, 10–12, 21–24, 28–29, 32, 34–41, 44–45, 47, 53, 64–72, 77–80, 82–85, 101, 106–107, 110–113, 116, 140, 152–153, 155–159, 172–176, 178, 180–199, 214, 216, 225, 229, 231–233, 235, 238

Grail, 198

Grain, 2, 43, 46–47, 60–61, 102–103, 158, 161, 175, 196, 198, 201

Greenman, 160–161, 184

Harvest, 41, 43–47, 63, 96, 99, 107, 158–159, 161, 172–173, 175–176, 184, 190–192

Harvest Lord, 44–46, 158–159, 161, 172–173, 184, 190

Hearth, 12, 14, 18–25, 36, 102, 164

Hecate, 11, 24, 27, 71–72, 80, 84, 115, 199, 214, 232–233

Holly King, 43, 160, 175

Hunted, 5, 157–158

Hunters, 5, 157

Imbolc, 30, 34, 36, 40, 174, 178, 184

John Barleycorn, 158

Leland, Charles, 138, 216–217, 237

Life, ix, 3, 7, 15, 24, 28–29, 31–32, 36–40, 44–45, 49–50, 52–54, 61, 63–64, 70, 89, 92–93, 96–97, 99, 101–102, 126, 133, 137–138, 140–147, 150, 156–161, 163, 173–176, 179–188, 190–194, 204–211, 214, 237

Litha, 30, 43, 178

Lughnasadh, 30, 43–44, 176, 178, 190

Mabon, 30, 44, 178

Moon, ix–x, 7–8, 10, 15, 17, 24–25, 29, 31, 36, 43, 50–51, 59, 61, 63–67, 69, 74–77, 79–85, 103, 109, 111–113, 116, 128–129, 139–140, 143, 154–158, 173, 194–199, 232–233, 235, 237

Moonlight, vii–viii, x, 75, 77, 79, 81–83, 85, 87, 89, 113, 147, 197

Nature, x, xiv, 4–7, 10–11, 13, 17, 20, 23, 25, 27–29, 33, 36–37, 43–44, 48, 50–51, 53, 56, 59–60, 63, 67–68, 70, 74–77, 81,

84, 89, 95–97, 99, 102, 106–107, 116, 123–127, 130, 140, 142–143, 146, 150, 154, 157, 160–162, 164, 166, 169–172, 175–176, 184–185, 198–199, 203–205, 207, 210, 214, 233

Night Witch, 75

Oak King, 43, 160, 175

Pentacle, 48, 64, 66–67, 88, 105, 107–110, 126–127, 136, 194, 196, 223–224

Pentagram, 47, 109, 116, 142, 233

Proserpina, 24, 80, 82, 199, 233

Rebirth, 17, 21, 32–33, 36–38, 63, 70, 83, 138–141, 145, 147, 151, 155–157, 172, 174, 182–183, 186, 216, 227, 229

Reincarnation, 50, 161, 175

Ritual, 11, ix–xi, xiv, 7, 29, 32–35, 37, 39, 41, 43, 48–49, 53, 64–65, 70, 72, 77, 83, 85, 87, 100–101, 104–109, 113–115, 121–123, 125–127, 133–134, 139, 141, 159–160, 162–163, 169, 176–177, 179–196, 198–199, 223–225, 237

Sabbats, 30, 61, 65, 143, 167, 172–173, 175, 227

Sacred Space, xi, 106, 123, 179

Salamanders, 48, 124, 162–163, 232

Samhain, 30–32, 40, 46, 173, 178–179

Satan, 9–10, 27

Solstice, 29, 32–34, 43, 64, 144, 158–160, 164, 169, 172, 174–176, 178, 189

Spring, 7, 33–34, 36–39, 41–42, 45–46, 64, 82, 85, 98, 107, 128, 144, 146, 159, 170, 174–175, 178, 185, 196, 205, 207

Stag, 157, 175, 225

Summer, 7–8, 39–44, 64, 107, 144–145, 159–160, 164, 170, 175–176, 178, 189, 205

Summerland, 145–146

Sun, 15, 17, 22, 29, 31–33, 37, 40, 50, 63–64, 67–68, 70, 76, 79, 85, 105–106, 139, 147, 154, 157–160, 170, 172–175, 182–185, 189, 195

Sylphs, 48, 124, 162–163, 232

Transformation, 10, 21–23, 48, 70, 86, 122, 139, 145, 161, 198, 212, 232

Transition, 71–72, 175

Trees, ix, 5, 14–15, 17, 32, 37, 40, 67, 76, 81, 83, 98–99, 110, 145, 153–154, 160, 166, 182, 184

Underworld, 11, 13–17, 19–20, 23–24, 31–32, 36, 44–45, 63, 70, 79–80, 83, 106, 114–115, 139–140, 145–147, 155–157, 159, 174–176, 185–186, 192, 228, 231, 233

Undines, 48, 124, 162–163, 232

Wand, 48, 64, 88, 105–111, 126–127, 136, 194, 196, 224

Winter, 7–8, 31–34, 37, 39–40, 44–45, 64, 85, 107, 144, 147, 158–160, 164, 170, 172, 174, 178, 205, 207

Wood, 13–14, 18, 21, 33, 36, 41, 83, 109–111, 113

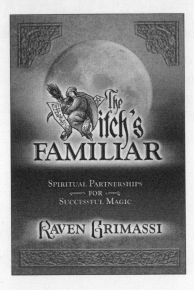

The Witches' Familiar

Raven Grimassi

Use them as guardians during dream/ astral work or to protect your home and property. Familiars can also aid in spell casting and other works of magick.

The Witches' Familiar is the first thorough and serious work on the subject for modern Witches and Pagans. It shows how to obtain a Familiar and work with one, and it also provides cautions and remedies for any problems that may occur in this magical partnership.

Learn a magical system for creating and using mystical seals designed to evoke Familiar spirits. This is never-before-published material, based upon Pagan elements rather than the more common Hebrew and Kabbalistic seals.

- Explores the three types of Familiars: the physical, astral, and spiritual

- Provides instructions for selecting a Familiar and a guided journey for finding one

- Includes "care and feeding" guidelines

- Explains how to work with Familiar spirits to cast potent spells

- Shows how to create magical seals to draw your desire and make magical images to house a Familiar spirit

0-7387-0339-7, 192 pp., 6 x 9   **$12.95**

Encyclopedia of Wicca & Witchcraft

Raven Grimassi

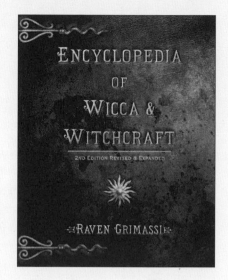

This indispensable reference work provides both a historical and cultural foundation for modern Wicca and Witchcraft, and it is the first to be written by an actual practitioner of the Craft.

Other encyclopedias present a series of surface topics such as tools, sabbats, Witchcraft trials, and various mundane elements. Unique to this encyclopedia is its presentation of Wicca/Witchcraft as a spiritual path, connecting religious concepts and spirituality to a historical background and a modern system of practice. It avoids the inclusion of peripheral entries typically included, and deals only with Wicca/Witchcraft topics, old and new, traditional and eclectic. It also features modern Wiccan expressions, sayings, and terminology. Finally, you will find a storehouse of information on European folklore and Western Occultism as related to modern Wicca/Witchcraft.

1-56718-257-7, 528 pp., 8 x 10, 300+ illus. & photos $24.95

Beltane
Springtime Rituals,
Lore & Celebration

Raven Grimassi

Beltane examines the ancient pagan origins of May Day festivals that thrived up to the end of the nineteenth century. Explore the evolution of the May Pole and various folklore characters connected to May Day celebrations. Discover the influences of ancient Greek and Roman religions on May themes arising in the Celtic cultures of continental Europe and the British Isles.

Beltane includes arts and craft projects, recipes for celebratory meals, and several spells related to the May themes of growth and gain. There is also a Beltane ritual for both solitary and group practitioners.

This well-researched book corrects many of the common misconceptions associated with May Day. It will help the reader more fully appreciate the spirituality and connection to Nature that are intimate elements of May Day celebrations.

- Learn the inner meanings of May Day celebrations, and make an authentic May Pole centerpiece for your Beltane festivities

- Cast spells for gain and success in harmony with the season of growth

- Perform a May Day ritual of alignment with the forces of Nature

- Explore fairy lore and flower lore dating back to nineteenth-century sources

1-56718-283-6, 192 pp., 7½ x 9⅛, illus.   **$14.95**

Hereditary Witchcraft

Secrets of the Old Religion

Raven Grimassi

This book is about the Old Religion of Italy, and contains material that is at least 100 years old, much of which has never before been seen in print. This overview of the history and lore of the Hereditary Craft will show you how the Italian witches viewed nature, magick, and the occult forces. Nothing in this book is mixed with, or drawn from, any other Wiccan traditions.

The Italian witches would gather beneath the full moon to worship a goddess (Diana) and a god (Dianus). The roots of Italian Witchcraft extend back into the prehistory of Italy, in the indigenous Mediterranean/Aegean neolithic cult of the Great Goddess. Follow its development to the time of the Inquisition, when it had to go into hiding to survive, and to the present day. Uncover surprising discoveries of how expressions of Italian Witchcraft have been taught and used in this century.

1-56718-256-9, 288 pp., 7½ x 9⅛, 31 illus.   **$14.95**

The Witches' Craft
The Roots of Witchcraft & Magical Transformation
Raven Grimassi

Enter the old forms of Witchcraft (many of which have been forgotten), and learn the ways and techniques that provide a solid foundation for further study, qualifying you to become the local village Witch! The material is selected for its authenticity, and demonstrates that Witchcraft is an evolving religion, not a modern construction.

Containing many aspects of Witchcraft never before seen in print, these pages will take you through the labyrinth of Witchcraft's history and deliver up the secrets of the Witches' craft, which lie deep within the center of the maze. It is a treasure worthy of pursuit.

- A serious and in-depth study of the old ways of Witchcraft
- The first book to present the entire unedited method of constructing the witches' ladder
- Examines the obscured roots of witchcraft from ancient to modern times, with historical and literary references
- Contains correspondence between the author and Doreen Valiente that sheds further light on the evolution of Witchcraft as it is practiced today
- Preserves much of what has been forgotten, misplaced, or discarded through the years

0-7387-0265-X, 312 pp., 7½ x 9⅛, illus.   **$16.95**